BY GOD'S Grace

HOW GOD LED US TO FAITH, THROUGH HEALING AND BEYOND

LAURA & MICHAEL KONDRATUK

By God's Grace: How God Led Us to Faith, Through Healing and Beyond
Copyright © 2021 CatholicShop Publishing

Written by Laura & Michael Kondratuk
Edited by Andrea Schmidt, Christy Bock and Amelia Chaplin
Cover Art by Karen Sheets and Amelia Chaplin

ISBN: 978-1-954438-00-2

Stella Mar Films & Catholic Shop Publishing
317 Riveredge Blvd, Ste 102
Cocoa, FL 32922 USA

www.stellamarfilms.com
www.catholicshop.com
info@stellamar.org
help@catholicshop.com
1-800-565-9176

About the Cover Photo

After our son Eric died, I walked and walked and walked...

One day, while walking in the nature park near our home, I suddenly noticed little sunflowers alongside the path. These are the same type of flowers Eric gave me on the day before he died. Whenever I see them, they remind me of Eric's generosity and sweet spirit. I quickly snapped this shot and saw how the sun's rays shone down upon them in the picture. This image helps me recall the graces God has poured on our family and the rays of God's love that continually inundate Eric's soul.

Laura Kondratuk

A Note From

Monsignor Charles M. Mangan

The Kondratuk have offered to us a kind of reflection: a moving meditation on the mystery of God's love and mercy. Mike and Laura, along with their children, Nathan and Katherine, experienced the tragic passing of +Eric that has not ended in a hopeless resentment, but rather in a fresh confidence in the God Who created us and Who saves us. The reader will find that the frequent reception of the Church's Sacraments and the fervent veneration of the Blessed Virgin Mary sustained the Kondratuk family during both joy and sorrow. May the same be said for all of us.

Monsignor Charles M. Mangan
Office of the Marian Apostolate
Diocese of Sioux Falls

Foreword

To forget is a kind of two-edged sword.

Thankfully, with God's abundant grace, we forget—or at least learn to accept—those indescribable hurts, pains, and sadness that are part of our lot here on earth.

Regrettably, apart from God's abundant grace, we forget the unspeakable blessings, joys, and graces that can only come from the generous hand of Our Lord.

The volume before you is all about remembering, accepting, and not forgetting. On page after page in "By God's Grace: How God Led Us to Faith, Through Healing and Beyond," Laura and Michael Kondratuk, who belong to Saint Thomas More Parish in Brookings, South Dakota, communicate the absolute necessity of recalling with gratitude the Almighty's goodness, and they take to heart the Psalmist's imperative: *"Remember the wondrous deeds He has done, His wonders and words of judgment."* (Psalm 105:5)

This book is a testimony to how Jesus Christ has shown Himself to Mike and Laura as well as to their three children, Nathan, Katherine, and +Eric. What we find is that, no matter the joys and sorrows, the highs and lows, the Kondratuks have experienced the Living God, especially through the reception of the Sacraments of the Church, particularly Penance and the Most Holy Eucharist, Eucharistic Adoration, the recitation of the Holy Rosary, meditation on Sacred Scripture, the wearing of the Scapular Medal, by performing acts of charity to one another and to the larger community, and by receiving love and kindness from many disciples of Christ.

The passing of +Eric was—and remains—a very difficult loss for the Kondratuks. Yet, they know that God has not abandoned them. And, they look forward to being reunited with their son and brother on the Last Day when the resurrection of the dead will occur and Everlasting Life in Heaven with the Most Blessed Trinity, Our Lady and the Angels and Saints will be the reward of the just.

Mike and Laura inspire us with their dedication to the Risen Lord Jesus Christ and His beloved Spouse, the Church, and their veneration of the Blessed Virgin Mary. How fitting that this work would be prepared during the Centenary of the Apparitions of Our Lady of Fatima.

May God bless the Kondratuks for sharing with us how He continues to move powerfully within them.

> The Most Reverend Paul J. Swain
> Bishop of Sioux Falls
> Solemnity of the Immaculate Conception
> December 8, 2017
> Centenary of the Apparitions of Our Lady of Fatima

Dedication

We dedicate this book to our children, Nathan, Katherine, and Eric. Thank you for teaching us how to love wholeheartedly and selflessly, and for teaching us how to be parents. Thank you for helping us to grow as we have been witnesses to your own growth throughout the years. May God bless you and lead you into ever-deeper relationships with His Son, Jesus. We love you beyond our ability to express it.

We also dedicate this work to Our Blessed Mother Mary, in thanksgiving for all she has done to help us become the people God created us to be. We are works in progress, but we know that she is with us, helping us along our journey with her Son, our Lord Jesus, and our Heavenly Father God.

Acknowledgements

No anticipation or presumption is made herein of the Church's final decision regarding any reported apparition or vision. We humbly submit and adhere to any future judgment by the Holy See regarding the Apparitions of Medjugorje.

We wish to acknowledge and thank Andrea Schmidt, Christy Bock and Amelia Chaplin for editing this work for us. Their patience, encouragement and suggestions for improvement helped us realize the completion of this project.

We also thank each person who encouraged us to write this book. Without your promptings, we never would have pursued writing down our experiences.

Thanks, as well, to all who have ministered to us in our need in any way and who have held us in their thoughts and prayers. May God bless you with a fresh outpouring of His Holy Spirit and love.

Preface

Laura

"You should write a book!"

We were attending a dinner party when a friend made this statement after hearing Mike share his conversion story. Mike and I love to share the powerful ways that God has acted in our lives. On many occasions after doing so, we've been encouraged to write a book. We've also come to realize that, by sharing our story, people who are struggling in their faith may find hope and reason to believe in God's love for them.

We are Mike and Laura Kondratuk. There's nothing special about us—other than the fact that we've been married more than 30 years. We're sinners like everyone else, and when we look back throughout our years together and see the ways God has acted, we don't understand why He has touched us with His grace. We're awestruck at God's love and power working in our lives. By sharing these experiences, we hope to show that God desires to fill with His love the emptiness in the souls of all of His children. We recognize that none of what we are about to share is a credit to us. As St. Paul wrote in his letter to the Ephesians:

"For by grace you have been saved through faith, and this is not from you; it is the gift of God; it is not from works, so no one may boast." (Ephesians 2:8-9)

We wish to give glory to God for the graces and blessings He has poured upon us. So, we're writing a book.

Part I

CHAPTER 1

Mike often says, "Before my conversion, if someone had come up to me and told me this happened to them, I would've listened politely and, when they were finished, I'd walk away, shaking my head and thinking, 'LOONEY TUNES!'" But we assure you, we're not "looney tunes." The events we describe here actually happened to us. They demonstrate what God can and will do to heal His children and bring them back to Himself.

We began our married life on August 8, 1986. For the first three-and-a-half years, we lived in a Chicago suburb. Then, we decided to move to the beautiful north woods of Wisconsin. Mike loves fishing, and northern Wisconsin offers some of the best fishing waters in the country. We both felt that the quiet, low-key lifestyle would be the perfect environment in which to raise the children we hoped to have.

After four-and-a-half years of marriage, we welcomed our first child, Nathan—our little five-pound, five-ounce siren-screamer. Two years and two months later, Katherine joined the family sporting the same little chin dimple as her big brother and, weighing just four pounds, twelve ounces, she was tougher than she looked. Then, after another two years and two months, Eric arrived to complete our family. He, too, had Daddy's chin dimple—along with Mommy's blue eyes—and was our biggest baby at seven pounds, fourteen ounces. We were amazed that, from the very beginning, they each had their own unique personalities. Nathan was very imaginative and loved stories—especially history—from an early age. He was a tenderhearted and fun-loving boy. Katherine was tenacious and feisty—yet sensitive, shy and compassionate. Eric was extremely independent and serious, but also had a great sense of humor; he had his dad's engineering mind and inquisitive nature, as well as his mom's musical abilities and caring heart.

. . .

Growing up, I attended Catholic school from fourth through eighth grade, which included Mass each morning. I always loved to sing and, while singing the songs in church, I felt close to the Lord. My relationship with God began to grow during those early years. In high school, a friend helped this relationship to deepen even further by giving me a Bible. I began spending time in the Living Word of God, and especially enjoyed reading the Gospels, Saint Paul's letters and the Psalms. In fact, I started to wonder if the Lord might be calling me to religious life and began checking into various orders. One night, a week before my birthday, I went out dancing with a friend and I met Michael Kondratuk. He was tall, handsome, fun, and friendly. Mike reminded me of John Denver, with a very cute chin dimple. Apparently, I made an impression on him, too, because one week later on my birthday, I came home from work and found a bouquet of flowers waiting for me. They were from Mike, and that's how we began dating.

On one occasion, while I was being visited by a nun from an order I was investigating, the doorbell rang. There stood Michael with a beautiful bouquet of flowers in his hands as the nun was sitting on the sofa in the living room behind me. How awkward! I realized that it was time for me to make some big decisions.

Being loved by Mike was like nothing I'd ever experienced. He loved me in spite of my many flaws. He was patient with my up-

and-down moods, and he was determined that our relationship would last in spite of my doubts that I could be the person he deserved. When I think of those days, I am reminded of the old song lyrics by Joseph McCarthy, "You made me love you. I didn't want to do it, I didn't want to do it."[1] My parents had a rocky marriage, so I really didn't want to get married—ever! However, Mike's patient, loving kindness and old-fashioned, gentlemanly qualities (after more than 30 years of marriage, he still opens the car door for me), and tenacity won me over; I realized that my vocation was to be his wife.

Our family around the time God blessed Laura with songs inspired by the Holy Spirit

I was busy with this vocation as Mike's wife and the mother of three small, energetic children—Nathan was almost six; Katherine, three and a half; and Eric eighteen months old—when, on February 26, 1997, I was blessed with an incredible outpouring of God's Holy Spirit.

As I looked out the patio doors of our home, I wished spring would arrive and melt the snow so the kids could get outside and burn off their excess energy. At that moment, the following words and a beautiful melody took shape in my mind:

> *The warmth of spring melts the snow away, as your Word warms my heart, and life springs forth upon the earth as it*

has done from the start.
Sap now rises into the trees, which will cause the buds to
grow.
Your Spirit rising up in me causes me to know:

That you, Lord, are the vine and we the branches, and all
who live in you will bear great fruit.
Yes, you, Lord, are the vine and we the branches, and all who
live in you will bear great fruit.[2]

"Wow!" I thought, "Where did that come from?" Although I'd studied vocal performance in college, I'd never written a song! Quickly, I began jotting down the words. More followed and, in one afternoon, a complete, three-verse song I called "Bountiful Harvest"[2] had formed in my mind. The next day, another song emerged, and again the day after that. I could feel the power of God surging through me as words and melodies poured from my imagination; I was merely an instrument through which He was creating. By May of that year, through this outpouring of the Holy Spirit, I had written 26 songs! I knew I wanted to call the body of work "Have Faith" because it was my faith in God that allowed Him to use me to create these songs, and because I wanted the songs to encourage the listener to have faith in God. Through the years, we have worked to create a CD of our favorites from this collection.

CHAPTER 2

Mike

I was born to immigrant parents—my mother was a German citizen from German-occupied Yugoslavia and my father was from Ukraine; when they came to America, they settled in Chicago. While Dad was of the Greek-Orthodox faith, Mom was Catholic, and they decided to raise my brother, sister, and me as Catholics. They encouraged our faith by enrolling us in religious education classes and required us to participate in church.

However, from an early age and until I was around 13 years old, I would always get sick during Mass—not the kind of sick that kids invent to get out of going to church. In fact, I'd actually feel dizzy and sick to my stomach, which would cause me to leave Mass. Then, strangely, I'd feel great once I was outside the church; eventually, I no longer attended Mass. I wonder if this situation was a symptom of the spiritual battle that we all endure in our earthly lives.

Another unusual example occurred when I was about nine years old. As children, my siblings and I often played cowboys, army, and even a devil game. One day, we were playing the devil game and I was running between houses chasing neighborhood kids and my younger sister. Then, suddenly, as I was running at full speed, I stopped. My legs went straight out in front of me and I levitated for a few seconds before falling to the ground and landing on my bottom. To this day, I wonder what forces caused this strange, scary experience.

Later, although I no longer attended church as a teenager, I did continue to pray—for my father, in particular. He was a heavy smoker, and I often heard him coughing loud and hard as he lay in bed at night. I was afraid he would die. So, every night, I prayed that God would allow my dad to live until I was at least 20. At the time, I felt that 20 years of age was old and that, by then, I'd be able to handle his death.

Then, the summer between my freshman and sophomore years at college, Dad died of lung and bone cancer. I was 20 years old. And, though he had lived until I was the age I'd prayed for, I certainly was not ready to handle it. Instead, my family and I now found ourselves in an extremely difficult financial situation and facing an uncertain future.

. . .

I've always had a very caring, compassionate heart, and am especially sensitive to mentally challenged people. For example, one day when I was about 10 years old, I was riding my bike at a park. I noticed a gang of kids taunting an older, mentally challenged boy whom I recognized from my neighborhood. The boy was crying as they shoved him, called him names, and laughed at him. So, I walked my bike into the group and, placing myself between the kids and the boy, I said, "Stop! Leave him alone." The boy left, and the group of kids turned their attention toward me—yelling, hitting, and kicking me until I was able to break free and run. When it was over, I went home with both my pride and my body bruised.

I was embarrassed because I didn't know how to protect myself. Mom fixed me up with a Band-Aid or two and tried to patch my bruised ego, as well. A few weeks later, I saw the same situation taking place once again. Without hesitation, I attempted to stop it and, this time, I escaped without injury. But, I was always looking over my shoulder, afraid of what would happen if the gang members caught me.

That's how I was before the spring of 2005—I spoke first, thought later, and was always on the defensive. I'd been told that I was not as smart as others and that I wouldn't amount to much. That I was too weak, too skinny, and so on. So, naturally, my self-esteem was extremely low. In spite of this—and probably to a great extent because of the difficult financial situation my family had endured—I worked hard. I graduated magna cum laude from high school, as well as magna cum laude from college with a degree in mechanical engineering. I did well in the business world, too, working my way up to become a director and officer of a nearly $70 million company.

Yes, life was looking good—except for the fact that I worked for and with unethical individuals. As a result, after several unsuccessful attempts to change their practices, I decided to leave that organization and start my own private company. To help finance the venture, I was forced to bring in partners, but a clash of personalities and goals made for an extremely stressful situation. Nonetheless, I carried the burden of the business because I had skills as a new product designer and also had relationships with our customers. So, I worked non-stop at the office and then again at home late into the night. Then, the next day, I'd get up early and do it all over again, even on the weekends. All this while my partners played Solitaire, golf, or even catch in the parking lot of our business. I was burned out, but people kept asking me to do more.

By this time in my life, I had never been close to the Lord. I did participate in church activities because I knew Laura wanted me to, and it was also important to me that I set a good example for our children. Even so, my standard line to Laura concerning church was, "Would you rather I go to church and think about fishing, or go fishing and think about God?" She knew I wasn't kidding. So, I split my time between going to church and fishing whenever possible. My priorities were as follows and in this order:

1. Work
2. Family
3. Health
4. Recreation
5. God/Faith

I was a spiritual wreck, but I didn't know it at the time. The stress of the business—and the personalities associated with it—became overwhelming.

That's when I had my first dream. In it, I found myself on a very rocky hill at twilight; I thought I had died! Questions began racing through my mind: Where am I? Why am I here? I'm in good shape, how could I have died? I was upset as I thought about my family. I wondered what they would do without me. I didn't know where I was or how I got there, but I felt as though I was physically in this place. I'd never seen anything like it.

Then, slowly, I was filled with euphoria. I realized that I was in the presence of something powerful, beautiful, and peaceful. My feelings and their intensity startled me. It felt as though my soul was before me. Looking around, I saw a tall, simple cross protruding from the ground among large rocks. In front of the cross were the dark shadows of people who appeared to be kneeling. I heard them chanting something, but I didn't see their faces. I also noticed a large statue of the Blessed Virgin Mary and felt the sensation of goose bumps. I was drawn to look at the face of the statue and, as I did, it suddenly came to life! Mary turned toward me, looked down at me, and smiled. I began to tremble and all of my feelings intensified.

In that moment, I woke up trembling and frightened. I had never experienced feelings or a dream like this before, and I didn't understand what had just happened. I woke Laura and tried to explain the intense dream to her. She thought the people chanting at the cross might have been praying the Rosary. This was new to me because, although I owned a rosary, I had never prayed one. In fact, although I'm a confirmed Catholic, the only prayer I knew at that time was "Our Father." As a child, I hadn't paid attention in religious education class; I much preferred to play army with anything I could get my hands on. I asked Laura if she knew what the dream could mean.

"I don't know, but I think you need to pray about it," she replied.

"What the heck is that going to do for me?" I asked.

So, I decided not to pray about it. But, for about two weeks, the experience was constantly on my mind. I just couldn't stop thinking about it. Truly, my soul was shaken to the core. Then, just when I had decided to let it go, I experienced a second dream.

Like the first one, in the second dream, I felt that I was actually present in the place I found myself—an expansive, overly crowded church. But, because of my experience with the first dream, I knew I wasn't dead. Instead, I was in the back of the church and people were packed in tight, elbow to elbow. I felt as though something important was happening and then, someone bumped me and I accidentally dropped my glasses. I dropped down on my hands and knees, searching for my glasses among the many feet in the crowd. Just then, I found them in front of a certain set of feet that looked different from the rest. The euphoric feelings I had experienced in the first dream immediately hit me like a ton of bricks and with high intensity. Instantly, I knew that these were the feet of Christ! I was before our Lord Jesus! I felt dirty, guilty, and unworthy to be in Christ's presence, and I couldn't look up to His face; rather, I just fell at his feet and wept. I was so moved that I trembled.

I woke suddenly to find myself in our bed—crying, shaking, and filled with an experience that, to this day, is still difficult to put into words. I felt as though I had stood before Jesus, and I was humbled in a way that I had never felt before. Shaking Laura awake, I told her that I'd had another dream. I recounted it at a hundred miles an hour, crying and trembling, trying to explain it to her. I wondered what was happening, why I was having these dreams, what they meant, and what I was supposed to do about it. I thought I might be going crazy! With thoughts like these racing through my mind, I paced around our bed when, suddenly, I stopped.

I turned to Laura and asked, "What does the word Medjugorje mean?"

She said she had never heard of it.

"This word just popped into my head," I said, "It's got to be something religious. You go to church all the time. Find out what it means!"

Shortly after this experience, Laura bumped into a friend, Judy Pottinger, who had just returned from a pilgrimage to Medjugorje, and she invited us to her home so that she and her husband, LaVern, could share their experiences. They introduced us to the little village of Medjugorje in Bosnia and Herzegovina, and shared with us that Our Blessed Mother has been appearing there since June of 1981. They told us about how their lives had been touched by God through those events.

Before we finished our visit, Judy said, "Mike, you should know that Satan's had you for a long time. He's not going to give up on you so easy."

However, I wasn't sure that I even believed in the existence of Satan, so I just shrugged off her statement saying, "Oh, I think I'll be just fine."

At first, I had my doubts and found myself reverting to my old ways—focused on work, stressed, and unhappy. But, after meeting with Judy and LaVern, I was convinced that I needed to go to Medjugorje, if for no other reason than to learn the meaning of my two dreams. The doubts persisted, and I remembered Judy warning me that the devil would use doubt to cause me to resist the urge to go to Medjugorje. Eventually, I signed up for a trip with Stephanie Percic, a tour guide who leads pilgrims to Medjugorje and, by then, had already led more than 90 trips. But, whenever a critical phase approached—such as a trip payment, preparation meeting, you name it—I had strong doubts.

Stephanie Percic began leading pilgrims to Medjugorje in 1983, and she has led more than 140 groups! Previously, Stephanie was a school teacher, but she felt called by God to leave her career and follow His will for her life. She has lived on faith ever since and, to this day, she guides people to Medjugorje in the hope that they will encounter Jesus through His Mother there. Stephanie takes her responsibility very seriously.

Before setting out on the pilgrimage, Stephanie said that I needed to learn to pray the Rosary and, because I'd never prayed the Rosary before, I asked Laura to teach me. Refusing to pray with her, I prayed it in the mornings as I drove to work. I also started fasting on bread and water on Wednesdays and Fridays. At the same time, I was aggressively working out—both cardio and lifting weights—and found myself feeling weak and very hungry on fasting days. And, while I stuck with the bread fast, I was eventually eating two large loaves during my fast and found myself actually gaining weight!

Stephanie on Apparition Hill

Another suggestion that Stephanie had was that I wear a blessed medal. So, about two weeks prior to the trip, I asked Laura if we had one and she told me I should buy one. Although I was known to easily drop large amounts of money on fishing lures and just about any other type of fishing equipment, I refused to spend money on anything religious! But, in a junk drawer in our home, Laura found a religious medal that had been given to her by a friend who had discovered it when she was digging in her garden. On one side of the medal was the Sacred Heart of Jesus, and on the other was the Blessed Mother holding Jesus as a young child. So, using a chain from a drain plug and a replacement snap ring from a fishing lure, I assembled the religious medal for my use. The assembled chain represented me—not flashy, but very simple. Then, at a Knights of Columbus meeting, I had our priest bless the article. I was all set for the trip.

However, as I began driving to the airport, once again, I had doubts and even thought about turning around to spend the time with my family instead. I heard a voice in my mind saying, "There's nothing to these dreams. You don't need to go on this trip. You're being selfish. You should be taking a trip with Laura and the kids, not spending this time and expense on yourself!" Then, I remembered what Judy had said about Satan not wanting to let go, and that I should pray the Rosary whenever I felt his presence or influence. So, I prayed the Rosary and made it to the airport off-site parking. As I traveled on the shuttle bus to the main terminal, an inner voice kept encouraging me to turn around and head home, but I persisted as I walked into the terminal. Standing in the ticket counter area, I looked down the long row of counters and felt like a fool; I was wearing an identifying name badge for the pilgrimage tour and thought I looked like a dork. I was about to leave when a little older lady who reminded me of my mom appeared. She noticed my tour badge and her eyes lit up.

"Oh, I'm so happy to see you!" she said. "I was afraid I wouldn't find our group!"

Well, I couldn't just leave her when she was so happy that she'd found me, so I waited with her for others from the group to arrive. Once more people had joined us, I was again preparing to leave when I noticed that there seemed to be some tension between Stephanie and an airport employee. The employee was telling Stephanie that her group needed to check in at a different location downstairs. This was new and uncomfortable for Stephanie, who was trying to maneuver the situation so they could check in the way she was accustomed to. Fortunately, as part of my career, I had become a seasoned traveler and was very comfortable navigating through airports.

"It's okay, Stephanie," I said. "I've checked in downstairs many times. Follow me."

I showed everyone the way to the check-in at the lower ticket counter and found myself on the flight to Detroit. But, once again, on the flight to Detroit for the international connection, I continued to have persistent thoughts that there was nothing to these dreams. I thought I was being selfish and that I should turn around and go home to my family; I decided that I would let Stephanie know that I needed to return home as soon as we landed in Detroit. When we landed, I got off the plane and found her speaking with a group of tour members. I waited to break in and let her know about my change in plans. So, imagine my surprise when Stephanie turned to me and asked if I could help another tour member with her carry-on luggage.

"Sure, I'll help," I said.

My willingness actually resulted in me carrying a total of three women's carry-on bags, as well as my own. And, once again, many in the group were unsure of where to go in the busy airport, so I led the way for a second time. I figured that I'd make sure everyone got situated on the plane, and then I'd make my escape. As we moved together in a group, I felt like a mother hen with her little chicks following; these ladies wouldn't let me get three feet ahead of them! Once they were settled on the plane and all the luggage I had carried for them was finally stowed away, I turned to leave and saw the flight crew closing the plane door. So much for turning around! There I was, the reluctant pilgrim, on my way to Medjugorje.

During the flight, I went to chat with Stephanie. She was excited to share that, at the airport in Zagreb, we would meet a priest who could "read souls," and that she would have the priest read my soul.

Alarmed, I said, "Stephanie, I don't want anyone reading my soul!"

"Oh Mike," she said, "it will be such a beautiful experience!"

The suggestion made me feel panicky; I didn't want anyone to see the dirtiness of my soul! But Stephanie was persistent that it would be good for me and, unable to convince her otherwise, I excused myself and went back to my seat. Frantically, I began praying the Rosary over and over that, somehow, we wouldn't run into this holy priest. When we arrived at the airport in Zagreb, we didn't find him. Later, we learned that the priest was there when we were, but we'd missed seeing him—despite the fact that Zagreb was a very small airport. I realized that my prayer had been answered.

The first morning in Medjugorje, Stephanie described our daily schedule. A typical day would begin with morning prayer, followed by breakfast, and then off to the English Mass at St. James Church at 10 a.m. After Mass, we'd participate in various spiritual experiences, such as healing Rosaries, Stations of the Cross on one of the local hillsides, or listening to talks given by one of the priests or visionaries in the village. Then, we'd meet for dinner, after which we would again gather at the church for Rosary prayers, followed by the pilgrim Mass (in Croatian) every night at 6 p.m. After that, there would be Eucharistic Adoration, Veneration of the Cross, or a healing prayer service for about an hour.

I didn't say anything, but thought that this was definitely *not* for me; I had a hard time even going to Mass once a week! "This is ridiculous!" I thought. "Isn't it *illegal* to go to Mass more than once a day?" I didn't know anyone in the group, so I kept these thoughts to myself as I wondered what on Earth I was going to do with myself for 10 whole days.

St. James Church in Medjugorje

That morning, as I was walking with a group of pilgrims through the fields to Mass, people suddenly stopped along the path. A little group was gathered together, hovering above something on the ground, taking pictures, and exclaiming excitedly. I glanced over and saw a piece of reddish-orange yarn lying on the ground. I couldn't imagine what the excitement was all about. "It's just a piece of yarn," I thought.

Someone asked, "Aren't you going to take a picture?"

"No," I replied. "Why would I want a picture of a piece of yarn?"

After the pilgrimage, someone sent me a picture of what they'd seen. What I hadn't seen lying there in front of me was that this little piece of reddish-orange yarn had somehow come to be positioned in the shape of Christ's body on the cross. When I saw it later, it was as plain as day. But, at the time, without a strong faith, I couldn't see it.

When I participated in the Mass on that first morning, I was surprised to find that I actually enjoyed it and was very joyful! Afterward, we walked behind St. James Church to see the Risen Cross, a bronze statue that spans about 20 feet lying on the ground; the body of Jesus is lifted up from the cross and stands upright with his arms outstretched. Interestingly, the right knee of this statue began secreting a watery

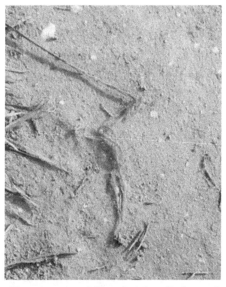

Picture sent to Mike after the pilgrimage [1]

liquid shortly after it was erected, and some people have been healed when they prayerfully came in contact with this liquid. As a result, pilgrims go up to the statue and wipe handkerchiefs over the place where the drops form in order to carry the healing gift to those who need it.

I hung back about 30 feet, letting others take turns going up to get swabs of the liquid from the statue. I was quite skeptical of the validity of this miracle statue; my engineering mind began to scientifically formulate an explanation for the droplets forming in that location. "Okay," I thought, "Let's be real. It's a bronze or copper statue, it's November, and it was pretty cool last night. I think they're all just wiping up condensation." Then again, I thought, if it was just condensation, there would be droplets in other locations, too. Next, I looked to see if there was a water fountain nearby. "If I can find one," I thought, "maybe they have a water line hooked to the knee somehow?" Nope, I couldn't find one. I had just ruled out these hypotheses—discovering no explanation—when it was my turn to go up and get my swab.

As I took the first step toward the Risen Cross, the feeling I had experienced in the second dream—when I was in Christ's presence—hit me like a lightning bolt! I felt my soul open up to God. I felt love, humility, and a great reverence. I began to tear up so much as I moved toward the leg of the statue that I could hardly see what I was doing! Then, after wiping my cloth on Christ's leg, I sat down away from the group, trying to deal with these overpowering emotions and crying like I've never cried in my life.

The Risen Cross. Photo taken by Mike as he was trying to determine the origin of the weeping at the knee.

Normally, I'm not one to show emotion. I didn't even cry openly at the funerals of my parents! But, at that moment, I couldn't help myself and I felt an intense need to go to confession. It had been at least 30 years since I had made my first (and last) confession. I looked for Father Albert, the spiritual director and priest for our group, but he was in deep prayer, and I didn't want to disturb him.

Once again, I began having doubts and persistent thoughts that I was making something out of nothing, that I was imagining the whole thing, and that I was just suffering from jet lag. I thought that I just needed a good meal and some sleep and I'd be just fine. Convinced by these nagging thoughts, I stopped crying, but I still wanted to go to confession and was watching for Father Albert when Stephanie mentioned that we were moving on to another location. Lagging behind the rest of the group, I seriously considered either going back to my room to get some rest or into town to get something to eat.

Then, a few women from my group stopped and turned back to look at me. I thought they might be concerned about me, so I started walking slowly toward them. One of them, Elizabeth, walked back to me and started walking with me. She said that she saw something at the Risen Cross that she felt she needed to share with me. She explained that, sometimes, when she is in deep prayer during Eucharistic Adoration, she sees the Eucharistic host glow. I must have had a puzzled look on my face because she asked if I knew what adoration was.

"No, I have no clue," I said.

She explained that Catholics believe in the real presence of Jesus in the consecrated communion host, and when a Catholic priest prays the Mass, the communion host (bread) actually becomes the true presence of Jesus during consecration. Then, during Eucharistic Adoration, a consecrated communion host—which Catholics believe is the body and blood of Christ—is placed in a beautiful container called a monstrance, which is placed on the altar for the faithful to come adore the Lord and pray in the presence of Jesus. During our time at the Risen Cross, Elizabeth said she was in deep prayer with her eyes closed when she opened her eyes and saw a brilliant glow all around the statue—much like the glow she sees around the host during Eucharistic Adoration.

"Mike, it was beautiful!" she said.

She also said she saw a separate light coming from the side.

"I thought you should know, Mike, the light was around your head as you were walking up to get your wipe," she said.

I was amazed; that was the exact moment that I had felt the intense feelings from my second dream, and no one could have known what I was feeling as I walked toward the statue. This was the confirmation I needed to know that what I was experiencing was real. I wasn't just imagining this, and I wasn't just overly tired from jet lag. I nodded to Elizabeth and walked away, trying to take in the significance of what had just happened. In that moment, I prayed from my heart the sincerest prayer I had ever prayed: "God, I don't understand what's happening, but I accept that this is real. Teach me what I need to learn. Show me what I need to see."

That evening, we went to St. James Church for the Pilgrim's Mass, where each evening before Mass, the people join in praying the Rosary. As we prayed, I began to sense the same euphoric feeling that I had had in my first dream when I stood before the living statue of Mary. The feeling began as it had in the dream— very faintly at first and then progressively stronger. As I felt the goosebumps intensify, I knew that the Blessed Virgin Mary, Mother of God, was there in St. James Church! I felt her presence for several minutes before the feeling slowly began to dissipate and eventually disappeared.

By then, I had noticed that the crowd had stopped praying the Rosary and was proceeding to pray again. Later, I would learn that every evening during the Rosary in Medjugorje, Our Blessed Mother appears to one of the visionaries somewhere in St. James Church. When this happens, the people stop praying the Rosary during the apparition and then resume when it is finished; I didn't know this when I felt her presence.

After Mass, I trailed behind some of my group as we walked along the dusty path through the vineyards and happened to look toward Apparition Hill. There, on the hill, I saw what appeared to be a large, illuminated Blessed Mother with a candle on each side. It reminded me of the inflatable characters you see in people's front yards during the holidays. I thought, "Wow, I didn't know they had one of those up there! That's neat!"—but I said nothing. The next morning at breakfast, I overheard some women talking with Stephanie about the beautiful, illuminated Blessed Virgin with candles that they had seen up on Apparition Hill the night before on the walk back.

"There is no illuminated Blessed Mother statue like that up there," Stephanie said. "There's no electricity up there! What you saw was a miracle!" (Electricity would be installed on Apparition Hill at a later time.)

The second day, I still felt the need to go to confession in the worst way, but I wasn't able to because the group was always on the go. Finally, as Eucharistic Adoration began after evening Mass, I took the opportunity to leave the church and go to confession, and I walked outside the church to the long line of confessionals. There were language signs on each of the confessionals and a light that reminded me of a doorbell. Some of the rooms were also lit from the inside, and I was confused. Would the interior light go on when I entered? Was the doorbell light the indicator that someone was inside? Feeling frustrated and with no one to ask, I decided to walk to the Risen Cross and pray. "Lord, I really want to go to confession, but I don't know how it works!" I prayed. After some time, without sensing an answer to my prayer, I felt I should go back to try again. When I returned, I found one man standing in front of a confessional marked "English." I stood back about ten feet behind him, facing away, and trying to act nonchalant.

The man turned to me and said, "So, you want to go to confession?"

"Yes," I replied.

"Here, take my place," he said as he looked down toward his feet where he stood, and then walked away.

Soon, the door opened to the confessional, the person inside left, and, at last, I had the chance to give my confession. As I did, I felt a variety of emotions. The priest, who was from Massachusetts, helped me by going through the commandments and asking questions. My confession lasted about 30 minutes. Afterward, we talked about my eating two large loaves of French bread on fast days and how I was actually gaining weight, and we spoke about the influence of Satan in my constant desire to turn around and go home rather than continue to Medjugorje. The priest told me that Satan is like a pesky mosquito and that we can send him away by saying from the heart forcefully, "I reject you Satan, I submit my soul to Christ. Leave me now!" He also said that Satan cannot enter us unless we let him, but he can continue to influence us and, therefore, we must be aware and strong to resist his temptations.

"He's had you for a long time," Father said. "He's not going to give up easily."

We spoke of my dreams, and I told the priest that, from where I was staying, Apparition Hill was about a quarter of a mile away. I told him how, at times, I could easily see a large statue on Apparition Hill but, when I searched for it at other times, I couldn't find it. I shared that I had this strong desire to go up the hill and had been asking Stephanie about it, but she wasn't sure when the group would be able to go. I explained to him that I felt I needed to go up there, but that I also didn't want to deviate from the group and offend Stephanie.

"When the opportunity presents itself," the priest said, "go up the hill privately so you don't create a distraction."

I walked out of the confessional feeling alive, peaceful, and renewed.

The third day of my pilgrimage began with an early breakfast, as Stephanie had planned for the group to walk to the home of Mirjana, one of the six visionaries (people who see the Blessed Mother Mary in apparitions) in Medjugorje. We arrived in front of her house at about 8 a.m. and the group prayed two Rosaries. During this time, Louie, a fellow pilgrim, suggested that I look at the sun. I was reluctant to do so after so many years of hearing how it would injure my eyes, but Louie insisted. When I looked up, I immediately noticed that there was no discomfort in looking directly at the sun! I also saw an inner disk that seemed to bounce within a circle of light rays around it. The rays were not from the circle, but rather just outside of the outer perimeter of a blue circle that surrounded the sun. I stared and realized that the sun looked exactly like the host in the monstrance at St. James Church during Eucharistic Adoration! I wondered if I could have seen this at any time, but just never had because I had always been told not to look directly at the sun. Because I also have a very short attention span, I became somewhat bored and looked away as I still doubted whether this was healthy for my eyes. I then closed my eyes and continued praying the Rosary. Later, I opened my eyes and noticed my rosary had turned a bright, brilliant shade of gold where my finger was touching the chain. Immediately, I thought I had burned my retinas and panicked. "What good is a blind engineer?" I thought. I began testing my eyes by looking forward and using my peripheral vision to see if the color moved—thinking that, if it did, my eyes were burned. But the color remained only on the chain where my finger was positioned.

Then, I tried to move my eyes in every direction, testing for confirmation that I hadn't damaged them, but only the gold chain remained. Moving my finger around, I noticed that wherever I placed it, the chain turned brilliant gold. I kept testing this and couldn't explain what was happening, so I continued to play with it, moving my finger around and watching the chain change color. When my finger moved away from an area, the chain turned back to silver, but it turned gold in the new position. I also experimented to see if the cross or medal would turn gold, but they didn't; only the connecting chain links turned pure gold. I thought about showing Louie but, for some reason, I felt that this was a sign meant just for me and that I should take it as a personal gift. Although I've never had an official diagnosis, I believe that I've always had attention deficit disorder, and after about five or ten minutes, I became disinterested even in this amazing phenomenon. So I closed my eyes, and continued praying with the group. When we were finished, my rosary chain was silver and has remained silver ever since.

After Mirjana's talk, our group went to Mass and I sat with my roommate, Kevin. A bishop from Canada who had blessed our tour group on the first day of the pilgrimage was presiding at the Mass, which was beautiful. When Mass was over, we had some time to explore on our own, so Kevin and I went shopping and, at one of the many vendor stands, I bought a holy water font for Laura. By the time we got back to our hotel, it was 2 o'clock and dinner was set for 3:30. I wanted to go up Apparition Hill, but because I didn't want to rush it, I decided I'd go after dinner, instead, and miss the evening Mass. So that afternoon I went to the Blue Cross—a spot at the foot of Apparition Hill where the Blessed Mother often appears—and caught up on my journal. It was very peaceful.

After dinner, I went back to climb Apparition Hill toward the large statue I had seen. At the time, I didn't know that there were pathways to climb the rocky hillside to the statue, so I just went to the foot of the hill and plunged into the rocks and brush. It was a difficult climb and when I arrived at the top, I noticed that the hill was crowded with people. I saw a simple cross and a statue of the Blessed Mother Mary. Finding a nice rock to sit on and facing the village, I closed my eyes and prayed the Rosary.

Mike with the statue from his dream

When I finished praying, I opened my eyes. Everyone had left and I was completely alone at twilight. I turned around on the rock and there I saw the *exact* vision that I had experienced in my first dream—the simple cross protruding from the rocks and the statue of Our Blessed Mother Mary. Where I had seen shadows of people kneeling and chanting in my dream, I now noticed memorial plaques that locals had placed in remembrance of their deceased loved ones. As I marveled at this view of Apparition Hill, I actually laughed out loud. Now, this was a true confirmation of my calling to Medjugorje.

"Thank you, Mary, for bringing me back to your Son!" I said. "Thank you, Jesus, for the signs and wonders you've shown me here. I am back! I don't need to see any more signs or miracles."

Almost immediately, a ball of light came from behind me and shot out just over my head straight between the cross and the statue. Again, I laughed. I was completely at peace. From that point on, I didn't experience any other miracles.

I returned to my lodging in time for a healing service with Father Albert. Although I had never believed in "resting in the Spirit," I was in for a special treat. Two fellow pilgrims and I were appointed "catchers" to actually catch people who collapsed after Father anointed them. Near the end, when everyone had gone except for my fellow catchers and me, I encouraged them to go first, saying it would never work on me.

"Humor us," they said. "It will take both of us to catch you if you do rest, so you should go first."

Then, when Father Al anointed me with oil, I tipped down instantly and rested with ease. And, while I didn't experience a vision, I did feel very peaceful. Afterward, everyone was hugging and I didn't miss a single person. It was a most beautiful experience.

On the last day of the pilgrimage, our tour group took a trip to Siroki Brijeg, a beautiful Catholic parish tucked in the mountains near Medjugorje. It was in this location in 1945 that thirty-four Franciscan priests died in defense of their faith, and we were there to listen to a talk given by Father Jozo Zovko, who was the parish priest in Medjugorje when the apparitions began. As we waited for the talk to begin, a young woman came up to Father Albert asking for a blessing. Then, suddenly, she began growling, spitting, and trying to hurt herself and those around her.

"Mike, get over here," Father called. "I need you now!"

I quickly joined Father Albert and helped the woman lie down on a pew. Father was saying prayers for her with holy water, oil, and blessed salt.

"This woman has a demon," he said. "I'm going to pray over her. She may get violent; hold her hands and keep her from hurting herself or any of us."

Father Albert performed what he later called "a mild deliverance." I had never believed that Satan was real; while I knew there were people who did evil things in the world, I certainly didn't believe in exorcism or anything like it. At that time, I was in pretty good shape and could bench press well over 300 pounds. But, as I held down the woman's arms, it was all I could do to keep her under control. I couldn't believe this was really happening! The woman then slowly turned her face and looked at me, and I felt incredible evil staring at me through those eyes! Suddenly, her nose shrunk while her mouth and chin grew before it all immediately reversed and her nose became large while her mouth and chin shrunk. Shivers ran down my spine. "Oh, my God! This is real!" I thought and, with all my heart, I prayed the prayer the confessional priest had given me: "I reject you, Satan! I submit my soul to Christ! Leave me now!"

Then, someone came up behind me and said, "Let go! Don't touch her! The demon will come into you!"

I looked to Father Al, and although he was extremely focused on the prayers he was praying for the woman, he motioned with his hand encouraging me to continue holding her. So, I prayed even more intensely as I held on tight! After a while, the woman settled down and, because Father Al had to go up front to help Father Jozo with the blessing of the people, he asked me to keep watch over her.

"If the demon is still present, it will try to disrupt the talk," he said. "Can you please take her out if she begins to do that?"

"Yes," I replied.

A fellow pilgrim named Rick came and sat with me, and we watched her intently. Whenever she would begin to groan or make any sound, we'd pray together and she'd settle down. I didn't hear a word of Father Jozo's talk.

Afterward, Father Al came back and we took the young woman up to pray with Father Jozo. I helped support her during the prayer and helped set her down when she rested in the Spirit. Father Jozo had continued praying over the group of people standing in front of him, and I wanted to be prayed over, too. When it was my turn, he prayed over me for a few seconds and moved on. But, when I saw that he seemed to pray over others for much longer, I felt as though I didn't get the full experience, so I went in line a second time. From his expression, I think Father Jozo recognized my request for a second helping, but again he prayed over me, finished quickly, and added a nod of acknowledgment when he was done.

Mike and Stephanie Percic during his first pilgrimage to Medjugorje

By the time everyone else had boarded the bus for the return trip to Medjugorje, I was exhausted! I was heading for the bus when the young woman who experienced the deliverance ran up and hugged me. A couple from Italy joined us and, acting as interpreters, shared her story. The young woman was from Italy. Feeling as though something was wrong with her and that she needed to see a priest, she had driven a great distance to see Father Jozo. Later, Father Albert shared with our pilgrimage group that the girl told him and Father Jozo that she had visited a fortune teller; Father Albert and Father Jozo believed that was when the demon had entered her. I couldn't believe the difference in her appearance; she was a totally different person!

I received one last gift on my way home from Medjugorje. During the flight home, I was thinking about a conversation I'd had with my fellow pilgrim Louie about guardian angels. According to him, my guardian angel was with me all the time. "It would be neat if you could show yourself somehow," I thought. "Let me know that you're really here." My next thought was that I needed to turn on my overhead light so I could fill out my U.S. customs card. But the light came on automatically the instant I had this thought! Caught off guard, I looked to see if I had somehow caused the light to turn on, but I hadn't touched the control panel at all. After I filled out the card, I thought, "All right, guardian angel, if it's really you, I need the light shut off." And the light shut off! I felt confident that these were signs from my guardian angel letting me know that he was there.

CHAPTER 3

Laura

When Mike returned from his first pilgrimage, he was a changed man and had an aura of peace around him. He arrived home late on a Thursday night and, after sharing his experiences with the family, he asked me, "Is there Mass tomorrow?"

My jaw must have hit the floor. I was shocked! This is the man who had resisted going to Mass on Sundays and now he wanted to go on a weekday? So, we went together that Friday morning and Mike actually sang the songs. He had never done that before. Joyful tears seeped from my eyes and I wanted to shout, "Thank you, Jesus and Blessed Mother Mary, for Mike's amazing conversion!"

Mike

A couple of weeks after my return from Medjugorje, I received a call from Carol, a woman who had been on the same pilgrimage and was present during the deliverance experience with the young woman from Italy. After we engaged in small talk for a bit, she got to the point of her call.

"Mike, have you been experiencing anything strange since we returned?" she asked.

"No," I said. "Why?"

Carol said that she had once helped during a deliverance, too, similar to how I had assisted Father Al.

"When I got home, I started noticing strange things," she said.

She explained that she had had extremely negative thoughts. Then, one day, as she looked at herself in the mirror, her nose became big while her mouth and chin shrunk before it reversed. The demon had come home with her! Knowing she needed help, Carol went to a priest who prayed for her deliverance. Her description of her appearance in the mirror struck me—I hadn't shared with anyone what I'd seen happen to the woman's face during the deliverance in Medjugorje.

"Mike, you need protection," Carol said. "You need to get yourself a scapular or a scapular medal. Get one, have it blessed and be sure to wear it. Promise me you'll do that!"

Although I didn't know what a scapular was, I promised. Then, after our conversation had ended, I researched scapular medals online and was amazed. The medal that Laura had found for me in our junk drawer—the one that had the Sacred Heart of Jesus on one side and the Blessed Mother holding Jesus as a young child on the other and that had been blessed before my trip—was a scapular medal! The website said that scapulars are known to be especially powerful in repelling Satan.

I had thought about the deliverance since returning home. I wondered why Father Al had called on me to help, and I realized that the confessional priest had taught me the prayer to repel

Satan for a reason; I had been praying it like crazy during the deliverance. I had also been wearing my blessed medal, the scapular medal. God had prepared me to assist in this circumstance, both with these tools and with my strong, natural desire to fight off bullies. The entire experience confirmed for me without doubt that Satan is real, that we have to protect ourselves against him, and that the Lord will help us in our battles against this enemy.

Mike's scapular medal

Laura

After his experience in Medjugorje, Mike wanted me to visit, too. And, although I was intrigued by the idea, I felt a little concerned. So much had happened to Mike; what if nothing happened for me? I worried that I might feel disappointed. But, since then, I've learned something about pilgrimages—especially those to Medjugorje: The signs of God's love and grace that one experiences while on pilgrimage are for the healing of souls and for their conversion toward God. Unfortunately, there can be a tendency to get caught up in an effort to collect miracles, and a person could end up feeling cheated if they don't perceive anything happening while they're there. But, for some, the graces they receive aren't evident until after they return home. Some people receive healing—physical, emotional, or spiritual. Therefore, one should go with a humble heart seeking reconciliation with the Lord. Our Blessed Mother can then lead the person to her Son in the best way for that individual.

So, in spite of my misgivings, I went with Stephanie on a pilgrimage to Medjugorje for the celebration of Divine Mercy Sunday, the week after Easter in 2006. I wasn't disappointed. Rather, I was blessed to see the miracle of the sun and I witnessed a beautiful painting of the Blessed Virgin Mary appear to come alive while I looked at it! Then, on the last morning of my pilgrimage, I decided to climb Apparition Hill by myself very early in the morning. I wanted to thank Jesus and His Blessed Mother for the graces and blessings our family had received in this place.

It was dark when I went up the hill. Unlike Mike, I chose to go up an existing path—which was much easier—and, with my flashlight in hand, I prayed the Rosary as I climbed. When I got to the top of the hill, I sat at the foot of the statue of Mary that had played such an important role in Mike's conversion. I was the only person there. As I finished praying the Rosary, I gazed up at the face of the statue, which suddenly appeared to change! In its place, I saw a man's face with bushy eyebrows and the name Peter popped into my mind. Then, I saw a series of women's faces, and I thought they might be saints. Next, I saw Jesus' face with the crown of thorns around His head. I could feel His love for me! Last of all, I saw what I knew to be Our Blessed Mother's face. It was not the face of the statue, but I knew it was Mary. As she looked at me with such tender love, I felt her motherly love for me.

I am the second of four children. At times while growing up, I felt neglected and carried a deep hurt in my heart. But, in that moment, looking at Our Blessed Mother's face and feeling immersed in her love, I was healed from this hurt. I heard the words, *"Trust. Be not afraid!"*

The sun was just beginning to rise as this experience ended, and I can't begin to describe the feeling of peace that filled my heart. It seemed to me as though I had been given a taste of heaven! To record this miraculous event, I took pictures of the statue and some flowers as I made my way back for breakfast.

When I arrived home, Mike put my pictures on the computer and we viewed them. Our son Nathan noticed something.

"Look at the eyes!" he said.

In several of the photos, the eyes of the statue appeared to be alive and Mother Mary seemed to have a gentle smile. This was a final gift that really gave us strength to face events in our future.

Two of Laura's photos—taken seconds apart—of the statue on Apparition Hill after hearing the words, "Trust. Be not afraid."

We didn't know how important the words, "Trust. Be not afraid." would be to us, but we would hold on to them with all our strength in the months and years to come.

CHAPTER 4

Laura

After Mike's first pilgrimage, he came home filled with the Holy Spirit and wanted to find ways to continue growing in his relationship with the Lord. Without even knowing what it was, he attended the National Catholic Charismatic Renewal Conference, which turned out to be an opportunity to learn about the Holy Spirit and the gifts of the Spirit. Later, he would learn that God hadn't just brought him to the conference to introduce him to the renewal; He was also setting in motion an opportunity for healing.

Mike

On my first pilgrimage, I met a woman named Mary. I didn't really get to know her very well, so I thought it was strange when I kept receiving promptings to call her when I was in Eucharistic Adoration. I ignored these little nudges until, at the renewal conference, I heard someone in the crowd call my name. It was Mary! She came through the crowd and we greeted each other with a little small talk before going our separate ways.

"Well, that wasn't a big deal," I thought. "I wonder why I felt I should call her."

During the conference, there were breakout sessions that began with the leader of the session praying over the whole group. Then, anyone who felt tingling during the prayer was asked to take a seat and a group of prayer partners would gather around them and pray for a specific charism of the Holy Spirit to be heightened in that person. This was a new experience for me, and I thought it was all just too strange. So, even though I felt tingling in each of the prayer sessions, I wouldn't sit. Finally, during the last breakout session, my fingers were tingling when the leader was praying for the gift of discernment of spirits, so I decided to take a seat and see what would happen. A group of prayer partners subsequently gathered around me and placed their hands on my shoulders and back. As they prayed, I felt an extremely hot hand on my back; it was so hot that I later checked my back for a burn mark. When they finished, I quickly turned around to see who belonged to the hot hand and there I saw a tiny woman—a nun.

"Your hand was extremely hot!" I told her.

She smiled sweetly and said, "I didn't feel anything, but I've been known to do that."

Later that day, a friend and I arrived at the last lecture a little late, and the only places left to sit were in the front, so that's where we found our seats. As I sat down in the front row and looked around me, who should be sitting right next to me but Mary from my pilgrimage. As the speaker began his talk, I suddenly saw standing before me a silhouette of bright light shaped like the Blessed Virgin Mary. In the same moment, I also received words that I knew were meant for Mary in the seat right next to me. I didn't understand the message, and I thought that this couldn't be real. But, when I opened my eyes, the image was still there. Closing my eyes, I thought, "If this is real, be gone when I open my eyes!" And, when I opened my eyes, it was gone. Closing my eyes again, I thought, "If this is real, be there again when I open my eyes." Once again, when I opened my eyes, there it was! I searched for paper and a pen and, finding a business card, I jotted down the words and tucked them into my shirt pocket with no intention of giving the message to Mary; I thought this was just too weird! Needless to say, I didn't hear any of the lecture.

When it ended, Mary suddenly turned toward me and asked, "Mike, what did you see?"

"What do you mean?" I replied, trying to play dumb.

"Don't give me that!" Mary said, wagging her finger at me. "I know you saw something. What was it?"

I sat there for a moment before reaching into my pocket and handing her the business card.

"Here, Mary, I think this is for you," I said.

As she read the words, she began to cry.

When she finished crying, she said, "Mike, you didn't know this, but when we were in Medjugorje, I was in remission from cancer. When we returned, the cancer came back. In prayer, I've been asking God a question. You just gave me God's answer!"

As Mary's cancer progressed, every so often I'd get that familiar nudge to call her. It was always when she was at a low point and needed encouragement. Finally, Mary asked if I would be present when she was on her death bed and pray the Rosary with her. I promised that I would and, being a man of my word, I fully intended to see it through. But what I didn't realize was how hard that would be, and I began to dread having to fulfill this promise. I would have to look death in the face, and I realized that I was afraid of it. My dad had died of cancer when I was 20, my mom had passed away from a heart attack when I was 24, and I didn't think I was ready to deal with death again. Nevertheless, when I got the call that Mary was near death, I arrived at her home. Her family told me that she couldn't speak any longer, but when she still could, she had asked if and when I'd be coming. Being there for Mary and praying that Rosary for her was extremely difficult for me. However, later I understood that, by doing this, I'd been healed of my fear of death. I also realized that I'd been angry at God for the deaths of my parents and this anger was lifted, as well.

CHAPTER 5

Laura

Not long later, we participated in a Catholic Charismatic Renewal retreat at a local church. Here, we learned about opening ourselves up to the power of the Holy Spirit, whom we had received in baptism and confirmation. Gifts, or charisms, of the Holy Spirit are given to every baptized Christian, but it is up to the individual to fan the flame of Christ's love within them and use these gifts in the ways the Lord desires for building up His Church.

Mike

I continued to receive messages during Eucharistic Adoration, one of which had to do with a couple I'd met on my second pilgrimage to Medjugorje, John and Jami Meilahn. I knew the message was for them, but I didn't understand its meaning. Later, they invited us to stay at their home during a time when several Medjugorje pilgrims had gathered to put a new roof on Stephanie Percic's home. While visiting with the Meilahns one afternoon, we began discussing the fact that the Lord seemed to be giving me these messages. When they asked if I'd share some of them, I got my journal from our car and began to share some of the Psalm-like messages.

Then, I said to them, "I think this one's for you," and read the message.

Jami began to cry and John looked at the floor, saying, "I don't believe it! Read it again!"

I read the message a second time and John left the room. Laura and I looked at each other, wondering what was going on. When John returned, the couple shared their story. John and Jami had gone to Medjugorje in part to learn what they should do with embryos they had frozen for in-vitro fertilization. They had come to believe that these little embryos had the right to life, but they already had four children and weren't sure they could handle seven! While Jami wanted to give them a chance at life, John wasn't sure it was a good idea. The message I had received was, "All must be done for the life of a child. Preserve life sincerely. Blessings will pour from large families. Rejoice and be glad for the gift of life. Follow me and my path, though it does not appear easy. I will lead and be with you."

So, John and Jami decided to implant all three embryos. As often happens, one embryo died when thawed and one did not make when it was implanted. And, although Jami did become pregnant with one of the embryos, there was a problem. Throughout Jami's pregnancy, both John and Jami were encouraged repeatedly by many members of the medical profession to abort their baby because they said she would be severely mentally disabled and have a terrible heart defect. But the couple refused this advice and were blessed with a beautiful daughter they named Madeline, a lovely child with Down syndrome. Maddie was born with a very minor heart problem and minimal level of disability; John and Jami's tenacity to save their child's life in the face of mounting pressure to abort was inspiring. As a result, many hearts and minds were changed to see the value of every life.

John and Jami Meilahn and family[1]

John and Jami's children and our son Nathan[1]

Laura

We were just beginning to learn about the gifts of the Holy Spirit and to recognize how God used these gifts through us. It was awe-inspiring! One of the gifts that Mike recognized in himself was the gift of discernment of spirits. Specifically, he can sense when various types of spirits are present in a given situation, like an especially sharpened empathy for a person's problems or feelings

Mike

In the meantime, the situation at my workplace had deteriorated drastically. I was under a great deal of strain, so I decided to go on a second pilgrimage to Medjugorje to discern the Lord's will regarding the business I had started.

On the last day of this pilgrimage, three strangers each came up to me at separate times and said, "I don't know why, but I feel I must tell you that you need to leave your job!"

I received the message and was convinced until I arrived back at the Minneapolis airport, when doubts began to hammer away at me. How could I just leave a business I'd started—and into which we'd invested a good deal of money—when I was the sole breadwinner of the family?

I didn't even have a résumé prepared, let alone another job! No, I thought; this couldn't be what God wanted me to do. I would need more proof.

The morning after I returned from that pilgrimage, with the words of those three strangers still ringing in my ears, I walked into the office building of the company I'd built from the ground up. But, when I entered the building, I could feel evil. Because of the experience I had had with evil on my first pilgrimage, I could recognize its presence—and the feeling was unmistakable. I went into my office and closed the door. Then, for the first and only time at work, I dropped to my knees and prayed. "Lord, I don't doubt the messages you've given me about needing to leave this place, but I do doubt my interpretation of the messages. Please, Lord, if this is really what you want me to do, I need to hear someone say, *"Mike, I think you need to leave this company."* I got up from the floor, opened my office door and sat down at my desk when the phone rang. It was Laura.

Laura

When I returned from my first pilgrimage to Medjugorje, Mike and I decided to build a grotto down in the pine trees at the shore of the lake we lived on. It was a beautiful setting for the private, outdoor prayer space we wanted to create. Mike took apart the kids' old wooden swing set and used the large beams to form a cross. Then, I stained the wood and we set up the cross in a large mound of dirt surrounded by stone slabs. We placed statues of Jesus and Mary under the cross and planted flowers in the dirt of the grotto to complete the prayer space. It was lovely.

I was down at the grotto on the morning Mike returned to work after his second pilgrimage. He hadn't told me about the strangers coming up to him and telling him to leave his company; his doubt was so great that he didn't want to share the idea with me. But I knew of his difficulties at the office, and I was praying for him to find peace or decide what he needed to do to change the situation; it was obvious that things couldn't continue the way they were. As I prayed for Mike, a vision formed in my mind. I saw him as a big, beautiful, multi-colored kite soaring in a bright blue sky. Then, I saw the co-owners of his company pulling him down by the string. They pushed him to the ground, grinding him into the dirt and tying him down with dirty rags. Immediately, I knew that the rags represented their disordered feelings toward Mike and the terrible ways they were treating him. Next, I saw Mike leaving his company for a new one where the people let out his string and allowed him to soar. I could see their joy as they stood watching him fly high into that beautiful blue sky, and I could feel Mike's joy in being allowed to reach his full potential. In that moment, I knew I needed to call Mike and share this vision with him.

Mike

I answered the phone and could hear in Laura's voice that she'd been crying.

"Are you all right?" I asked.

"It's okay," she said. "It's a good thing." She then shared the vision she'd just had, saying, "I felt that I should tell you, *Mike. I think you need to leave this company.*"

"I'll think about that," I replied as I hung up the phone.

And, although I was amazed that Laura had used the exact words that I had asked for in my prayer, I wasn't ready to commit to change just yet.

At that time, we were friends with a very holy priest from India, and I called Laura and asked her to contact Father to see if we could get together with him. It was the Friday before the Fourth of July weekend.

"Mike, Father must have plans for the weekend," she said. "I'm sure he'll be too busy to see us."

"If this is God's will, he'll find a way to make it happen," I replied. "If he's not available, that tells me something, too."

In my mind, if Father was unavailable or unwilling to see me, I would question which side the promptings were coming from. But, when Laura called Father, sure enough, he was free. We met with him that evening and he said that he would fast and pray to discover an answer to the question of whether I should leave. He said he'd call me with the answer on Sunday night. Father then said he had a very serious situation, which he shared, and then asked if I would fast and pray to help him know what he should do. On Sunday we talked as planned; I told Father what I had received in prayer for him and, Father let me know that he believed I did need to leave my company immediately. He said he sensed evil in my current workplace and that it was God's will that I leave. So, there were no more doubts. God had shown us His will, and I'd gotten exactly what I'd asked for. We realized this truly was what the Lord wanted for us, so I went to the office the following Monday morning—where I again felt the presence of evil—and gathered the co-owners together.

"I'm leaving the company," I said. "It's all yours now."

Tuesday was the 4th of July, and when I returned to work that Wednesday morning, I made the final decision that I would be done that very day. Going back to my desk, I packed up my things and left without a plan or even a résumé in hand. It was truly a leap of faith. As I was driving away from the company I'd founded, I asked God the big question: "Now what?" This was a very unusual thing for me to do; I always have a plan and like to know my next move. But, this time, I left it in God's hands. And, as always, He had plans for me that I could not have predicted.

. . .

I belonged to a walleye league, and on the Wednesday that I left my workplace behind, I was scheduled to fish with a retired man who usually went fishing at noon. I had never been able to go at that time before, but when I left work early for the last time, I gave him a call and we went out.

"We probably won't catch much at this time, but we'll give it a try," he said.

As we motored out, I watched the miracle of the sun, which was now a comfort to me. It was as though the Lord was giving me reassurance that He was with me.

At the end of my first pilgrimage on top of Apparition Hill, when I saw the vision from my dream, I said to the Lord, "I don't need to see any more miracles." And, I hadn't seen the miracle of the sun since then—until the morning after Laura returned from her first pilgrimage. I had noticed her looking out our bedroom window at the sun with a tear running down her cheek.

"Are you looking at the miracle of the sun?" I asked.

"Yes," she answered. "Come look at it. It's beautiful!"

But, after trying three times, I still couldn't see it! So, I went out into the hall and prayed, "Lord, I know that in Medjugorje I said I didn't need to see any more miracles. But, if I could share this moment with Laura, I'd really appreciate it. If it's not your will, though, I accept." Then, I walked up behind Laura, put my hands on her shoulders, and tried to look at the sun again. This time, I saw it! I could look at the sun and it didn't bother my eyes! Ever since that moment, whenever I look to see the miracle of the sun, I can see it. I believe the Lord gives me this grace because He understands that I need reassurance.

So, as I watched the miracle of the sun while sitting in that boat, I knew the Lord was with me. I prayed, "God, if it doesn't go against your pure will, give me a sign that I did the right thing by leaving my company." Immediately, I caught an eight-pound walleye—my biggest to date! I felt like God was letting me know that, yes, I was doing His will.

After that, we prayed a lot, but God didn't seem to be showing us exactly what to do next. So, a couple of weeks later, I decided to write my résumé and start making calls to find work. One of the contacts I made was to a company I had worked with for many years. Although I wasn't their employee, they knew me very well as I had designed products for them. We'd had a great relationship, and I was hoping they'd give me a reference. But, instead, their management was interested in hiring me and made an offer! However, the job required a move and, because we had such deep roots in our community, I still had doubts. I really thought the Lord would allow us to stay in the town where we had lived for more than 17 years. We loved living there; our home was on a beautiful little fishing lake, which was a dream come true—especially for Nathan and me. Our roots were deep, our children had friends they'd known for all their lives, and we loved our church family and community friends. I couldn't believe that God was calling us to leave this all behind to follow His will, so I looked for other work opportunities. But each time I had an offer from a company that would enable us to stay put, I prayed, "Lord, I want to follow your pure will. Please, open the doors that need to open and close the doors that need to close for your will to take place." And, in each instance, the job opportunities that would have kept us in Wisconsin fell through.

Meanwhile, the company outside of Wisconsin grew impatient with my indecision. They invited me to come for another visit and suggested that I bring my family so we could explore the city together to help us finalize our decision. So, we prayed for God to give me a sign if this was where I should go to follow His pure will. While I visited, Laura and the kids played at a nearby park. But, after I had visited again and had still not yet accepted the position, the president and founder of the company took a moment to speak with me. He said they didn't have a position for me at this time, but they really wanted me to come work for them, so they decided to create one for me. He said they valued my integrity and talents and wanted me to come on board.

"You know, Mike," he said, "the way I see it, *you are like a kite. We want to let out your string and allow you to soar!*"

When I joined my family afterward, Laura asked, "Well, what do you think? Is this the place for us? Did you receive any signs?"

"Maybe," I said, and I told her about the president's kite reference.

Laura began to cry and said, "Mike, what more do you need for a sign?"

So, because that image fit Laura's vision, we took it as a sign that this just might be the right move for us. And, in September 2006, I started my new career in South Dakota—driving six hours from our home in Wisconsin on Monday mornings and returning home very late each Friday night to stay with Laura and the kids through the weekend. During the weeknights, I spent my time looking for housing for our family, but it was difficult to find something exciting for us, and I began to feel discouraged. We were giving up a newer house on almost two acres with a large pole shed on a small private lake...all for a house in a city with a small yard, and which required an additional $100,000—not very appealing or exciting at all. So, I'd go home to Wisconsin, go fishing, and enjoy the gifts that God had blessed us with there— then I'd wonder if we were doing the right thing. It was heartbreaking for me and Nathan to have to leave our lake, and I kept saying to Laura, "Maybe I should find something so we can stay here."

Laura

My nerves were becoming raw. While Mike was away during the week, I was packing up our belongings for the move. It was such a roller coaster ride, and I wanted to scream, "Are we going or aren't we?!" To make matters worse, the housing market in our area was depressed. And, because we didn't want to have two mortgages at the same time, Mike insisted that we sell our home in Wisconsin before we move. So, I began to pray a Novena (a nine-day prayer) to the Divine Mercy of God that our house would sell so we could have closure and follow the new direction that God seemed to want for us. Incredibly, on the ninth day of the Novena, our house sold! We were on our way. One particular Bible verse kept speaking to me at that time. It was Jeremiah 29:11:

> *"I know the plans I have for you, says the Lord; plans for*
> *good and not for evil, to give you a future and a hope."*

We held on tightly to the words, "Trust. Be not afraid."

CHAPTER 6

Katherine, Eric and Nathan just prior to our move to South Dakota

We moved to South Dakota on a bitterly cold day in January 2007. We ended up renting a Cape Cod-style house seven miles north of town in a wooded area—a rare find on the South Dakota plains. It was perfect for us and all of the trees reminded us of northern Wisconsin, making us feel more at home. While we worried about the kids having to start at a new school halfway through the year, we couldn't imagine Mike continuing the back-

and-forth routine for the rest of the school year, and his new employer really wanted us to begin making the town our home. Nathan was a sophomore in high school; Katherine, an eighth-grader, and Eric was in fifth grade. It was very difficult for Nathan, in particular, to leave the lake and his friends. He wanted to graduate high school in Wisconsin. Katherine, however, was excited about the move and the new opportunities it would bring. Eric was excited, too. So, we all dug in and began this new adventure together. Besides, there wasn't much choice in the matter; it was sink or swim and we decided to swim.

The kids found their new schoolwork slightly more difficult, but they were good students and adapted quickly. They even started making friends, although Eric had a harder time than Nathan and Katherine; plus, the school he attended had a tougher group of kids. On top of that, Eric felt sad because, in his old school, he had advanced into middle school by fifth grade. But, here, he had to go back to elementary, which was a blow to his ego. He began feeling downhearted and seemed to be having a tough time fitting in.

Laura

In March of that year, I was hired to work at the public library as a circulation assistant. Working at the front desk of the library was a great way for me to meet people from the community. In the meantime, we continued to look for a house before deciding to build one in town; we moved into our new house in August of 2007 and quickly became involved at the Catholic parish in our new town. Katherine and I sang in the choir, and Mike and I joined prayer groups and Bible studies, as well as the Catholic Charismatic Renewal group that exists in Sioux Falls, about an hour away from home. The children went to the Wednesday evening religious education classes, and I taught religious education.

Then, in 2008, Mike and I became involved in the Cursillo movement, which is very strong in our parish. The movement encourages members to grow in their relationship with the Lord and challenges them to make a difference in the world because of their faith. One aspect of Cursillo that has meant the world to us is that members are encouraged to join small prayer groups. Both Mike and I have been incredibly blessed by the relationships we've formed with our fellow prayer group members; they're some of the deepest friendships we've experienced as we've supported each other through life's trials. We're extremely grateful for the gift that God has given us by placing us in these small faith communities where we influence each other's lives for the better.

During my Cursillo weekend, when I first joined the movement, I experienced a vision during a private moment of Eucharistic Adoration. In it, I was three or four years old, wearing a pure white dress and walking barefoot up a grassy hillside. It was a beautiful, warm, and sunny day, and as I crested the hill, I saw Jesus coming toward me from the other side. I ran to Him and He lifted me up, swung me around, and sat down on a rock. He placed me on His lap, and I rested my head on His chest. I felt His love for me and was totally content and at peace. Then, as Jesus stood up and gently placed me on the ground, we looked down the hill in the direction from which I had just come. There were many other little children dressed in white running to Him, and I stood off to the side watching as He showed His love for each of them. I understood that He loved us all equally, and I accepted this without feeling jealous of Jesus' love—something I would normally find difficult. When Jesus had greeted each child, He motioned with both arms back down the hill. I understood that we were to take the love He'd given us and go share it. After this vision, I felt a great sense of peace and purpose. I knew that I had received incredible blessings and that I was now expected to share those gifts with the people in my life.

Around this time, in April 2009, Mike decided to go on his third pilgrimage to Medjugorje. He wanted to go and give thanks for all the Lord had done for him and our family; he calls this pilgrimage, "The trip of confirmations."

Mike

I had promised a friend that I'd go up Apparition Hill and pray for her and her husband at the statue of Mary upon my arrival in Medjugorje. And, although the tour group had arrived very late at night and I was extremely tired, I was determined to keep my promise. It was dark on the hill and, because it had been a while since my last pilgrimage, I'd forgotten the way to the statue. No one else was there to ask directions, so I continued searching in the dark. Suddenly, the hair on the back of my neck stood up as I sensed the presence of evil. I looked around and, about 100 feet away, I saw a dark mass that I sensed was looking at me. I'd been holding my rosary as I climbed the hill. Then I held it up in my right fist and shook it at the evil spirit. I saw it nod to me, and then it turned away and disappeared. I began to pray, "I reject you Satan! I submit my soul to Christ. Leave me now!" Taking a few more steps, I saw the statue about 75 feet in front of me! I went to it and prayed for the friends as I had promised, then I walked back down the hill to my lodging.

The next morning, as I sat in St. James Church waiting for Mass to begin, I was praying and thinking about some of the Eucharistic miracles I had heard about. For example, during a Mass in Lanciano, Italy, the presiding priest was doubting the real presence of Christ in the Eucharist and the Communion host turned into human flesh. I thought, "I already believe, so I know I don't need anything like that to happen." There were many priests at the altar of St. James Church celebrating Mass that morning. When the officiating priest held the host up during the consecration, I heard an extremely loud voice saying, "This is my beloved Son, in whom I am well pleased." The voice was so loud that it startled me! I looked around to see where it had come from, but as I looked, I realized that no one else had heard it. I listened more intently to the priest who was speaking and noticed that it wasn't his voice that I had heard. The other priests who had been at the altar when I heard the voice had all said Mass earlier in the week, as well, and none of them was the voice that I had heard. I believe I heard God speaking, confirming for me beyond a doubt that Jesus is truly present in Holy Eucharist!

Praying before Mass in St. James Church, Medjugorje

On my first pilgrimage, my rosary had turned gold in my hand. At the time, I didn't show it to anyone, but felt that this was a grace just for me. However, during this third trip, the thought crossed my mind that I should have shown it to someone to verify that it really happened. But, then again, I knew that it did; it was just a slight doubt that entered my mind for a brief moment. Then, one day, I unexpectedly received confirmation of my vision. Along with two dear friends from the pilgrimage group, I had ordered custom rosaries to be made for family members at home. We picked them up and, having time before dinner, decided to go to a patio to sit in the sun and look at the rosaries. As we sat, I looked at the miracle of the sun and the two women from my group noticed. They asked if I was looking at it and I said yes, but they tried to look and they said they couldn't. So, I told them how when we had prayed with people at home, they could often see it. My friends then asked if I would do this with them, and we gave it a try. We prayed and then everyone was able to see the miracle of the sun. It was a joyous moment, after which we showed each other our rosaries.

One of my friends, Kristy, pulled out one of her rosaries and, finding it pretty, I reached out my hand and said, "Let me see that."

She placed her rosary in my hand and, as she did, it changed from a silver color to gold.

The other woman, Tori, said, "That just turned gold! Do you see it?"

Kristy said yes and Tori asked if I could see it, too. I responded with a yes and handed the rosary back to Kristy.

. . .

Later, our group went to hear the visionary Vicka speak. A large crowd had gathered outside her home, and Stephanie, who was up on the stairs with her, motioned for the members of our group to come join them. However, several of us were toward the back of the crowd and some members of our group wanted me to lead them through the crowd to the front. But I didn't think it was right to force our way through the others in the crowd to be up front where they, too, wanted to be, so I didn't move.

"Well, don't you want to see Vicka?" someone asked.

"Of course I do," I said. "But, if it's God's will, he'll make it happen."

So, I stayed in the back and listened to her talk while the others went up by Stephanie. Two Canadian men with another tour group happened to be staying at the same place as we were and one of them, Jacque, was in a wheelchair. After Vicka's talk, I waited until everyone else had cleared out so I could help him get down the stairs. As I was helping move the wheelchair toward the stairs, I felt a little tap on my shoulder. I turned around, and there was Vicka, smiling at me. She gave me a big hug and kissed me on both cheeks! She said something to me in Croatian, which I couldn't understand. Then, she began speaking with Jacque. Amused, I thought that, apparently, it was God's will that I meet Vicka!

On another occasion, a few people from the group were walking through the fields from our lodging to "the castle" to hear a man give his testimony: Patrick was a very rich car dealer leading an empty, careless lifestyle. His irresponsible behavior left a swath of pain and destruction in its wake until, one day, he was given a book of Our Lady's messages from Medjugorje. He read one message and felt in the depth of his heart that Our Blessed Mother was truly appearing in Medjugorje and that he needed to change because of it. So, Patrick sold his business and took the money with him to Medjugorje. There, he and his wife, Nancy, built a beautiful stone building in the shape of a castle. They intended the castle to be used as a retreat center. Patrick totally changed his life because of the Blessed Mother's messages. Now, he shares his conversion story and helps others come to the same decision that he did…to leave lifestyles that are offensive to God and to turn to Him to receive His forgiveness and peace.

The Castle Retreat Center in Medjugorje

By then, it was raining and my companions and I came upon Jacque and his friend in the field. Jacque's wheelchair was sitting on a concrete slab. His friend told us that he was going to the castle to hear Patrick's talk and, afterwards, he'd return to take Jacque back to their lodging; he was going to leave Jacque there because he couldn't get him through the fields in his wheelchair. Although I offered to help, Jacque's companion didn't think we could do it, so he went on his way. But I just didn't feel right leaving Jacque there by himself, so I told my group to go on without me.

"But don't you want to hear Patrick's talk?" they asked.

"Of course I do," I replied. "But I don't feel right leaving Jacque here by himself, and I've been to the castle. If God thinks I should be there during this trip, he'll make it happen later somehow."

So, they left me with Jacque. He was able to speak a little English, so we chatted and talked about our families. Jacque said an extensive prayer for my family, and we agreed to pray for each other. As we were talking, two young men showed up and asked if we needed help.

"Yes, would you mind helping me carry Jacque through the fields to the castle?" I asked.

They agreed and we went to work. I took the handles of Jacque's chair while they each took a wheel and, together, we carried Jacque to the castle in time to hear Patrick speak. Then, the two young men left and I never saw them again.

. . .

Late one night, several people in the pilgrimage group had a frightening experience. By the time I had returned from the Risen Cross, everyone had gone to bed, so I decided to take a shower so it would be free for my two roommates in the morning. While I was in the bathroom, I felt the presence of evil, so I began fervently praying in tongues—a gift that the Holy Spirit had given me after I had attended the National Catholic Charismatic Renewal Conference years earlier. Praying in tongues is a prayer language inspired by the Holy Spirit that helps me pray when I'm not sure what to pray for. It is a means through which God's power can be manifested in a given situation. Sometimes, it's an earthly language that the person praying may not recognize, whereas other times, it is in God's own language, which is powerful because evil cannot understand it. As I was praying, I heard a loud voice yelling, "MOM!" from the other side of the wall in the bathroom, but I just kept praying until I suddenly felt the presence of evil depart. Then, I took my shower and went to bed.

The next morning at breakfast, the three women whose room was on the other side of my bathroom wall were talking about the events of the previous evening.

A young woman came up to me and said, "You were awake last night. You got up in the middle of the night and you were praying."

At first I said no, I didn't get up to pray. But then, I realized that she was referring to my prayers in the bathroom. I learned that several people had experienced an oppressive spirit that felt like it was sitting on top of their chests, making it difficult for them to breathe. The young woman actually saw an evil spirit outside her patio door and yelled—this was the scream I had heard as I prayed in tongues. The young woman had prayed to the Blessed Mother Mary, asking her if I was awake and if I was praying. Specifically, she had asked for a sign through the chirping of a bird, and it was confirmed to her by this sign that I was praying! In this moment, I learned that the feelings I experience are real; it also validated the power of praying in tongues inspired by the Holy Spirit. Fortunately, although several other members of the pilgrimage tour experienced the oppression by the evil spirit that night, no one in my room did; I believe that the power of God working through my prayers helped protect my roommates and me. During this "trip of confirmations," God showed me over and over that He loves us and takes care of our needs.

Part II

CHAPTER 7

By the spring of 2009, we were enjoying our busy life—although, at times, we felt stretched thin. In April and May of that year, our Life in the Spirit prayer group offered a Pentecost retreat, a seven-week seminar that offered talks and small group discussions leading to Baptism in the Holy Spirit. It was an opportunity to stir up the flame of the Holy Spirit within the heart of a person who had already been baptized and confirmed in the Catholic faith.

Laura

In one of our small group sessions, I admitted that I had a problem in one particular area in my faith life—the ability to release to the Lord the safety of my children. I was unable to trust Him completely with their safety and, although I wanted to let go and believe that He held them and would care for their every need, I felt fear at the thought of anything bad happening to them. I felt compelled to hold them especially close, and I couldn't completely submit them to God. It was something I knew I needed to work on.

At one of the meetings, we took time to pray before Jesus in the chapel tabernacle and I experienced a vision. Again, I was a little girl dressed in white but, this time, I was being held by Jesus. I giggled as I noticed water droplets hitting us and I looked down to see where the water was coming from. It was then that I noticed that Jesus was standing on a rough, rocky outcropping that overlooked a great sea, and as I looked out upon it, I saw huge waves crashing into the rocky shoreline below us. There before us was a terribly powerful storm with dark gray clouds rolling in toward us. It was frightening to look at and I snuggled closer to Jesus, burying my face in His chest. I felt comforted and warmed by His love as I realized that I was safe in His arms no matter what the storm would do. I didn't understand the meaning of this vision until four months later when our hold on the words, "Trust. Be not afraid." would be put to the ultimate test.

. . .

Saturday, September 12, 2009, was a beautiful day—warm and sunny with no wind, which is unusual in South Dakota—and the temperature was around 70 degrees. A few weeks earlier, we had moved Nathan—now 18 years old and a freshman in college—into the dorms at South Dakota State University. Katherine, who was now a 16-year-old sophomore in high school, was away for her first dance team competition. So, Mike and I decided to take Eric fishing on Lake Poinsett. Eric was in a good mood that morning and greeted me in the kitchen with his sweet, silly happy dance and a big hug, resting his full weight on me.

"Eric," I said, "I'm not strong enough to hold you up!"

As I made breakfast, Eric helped by making a cooler full of lemonade while I put together sandwiches and snacks for us to take in the boat. At 14 years old, Eric was just beginning eighth grade but, for many months, he had been suffering from depression. His periods of sadness and withdrawal had been increasing, and it was hard to encourage him to get out and be active with us. We would ask him to come for ride bikes, go swimming, or for a walk, but he didn't have the energy and usually declined. Finally, he asked to see a doctor.

"I'm tired of being sad all the time," he said.

At that point, Eric's doctor was searching for the right medication for him, weaning him off of one drug and onto another. However, Mike and I had noticed that the second drug seemed to be affecting Eric in a negative way; he was more withdrawn, and the activities that he took joy in—playing his guitar, building Lego creations or puzzles, and riding his bike— weren't interesting him. Concerned, we asked his doctor about this, but he said it would take time for the new medication to be effective in helping Eric and that the effects we described were normal.

When our lunch was packed, Eric and I went to look at the roses growing in our front yard. He liked the scent of the white ones, while I preferred the pink.

"Let's go see if Dad needs any help," he said.

We went into the garage and found Mike hooking up the boat. While we waited, Eric hugged me, lifted me up, and swung me around so that my feet flung back and forth like a rag doll. He loved being able to do this now that he'd grown tall and strong.

On the drive to Lake Poinsett, we enjoyed listening to a CD Eric had put together. Finally, we arrived at the lake, and Mike began putting the boat into the water while Eric and I busied ourselves. I stood on the dock and looked around as Eric investigated the shoreline. Ever since he was a very little boy, Eric had always loved to explore the pebbles at the lake shores we visited and, true to form, he found some interesting stones there that day.

"These must be ancient stones," he said. "See how the edges have been worn off by the waves?"

Then, he brought me two little sunflowers that he had found growing along the shoreline (bringing me pretty flowers was another thing he had done all his life). We enjoyed our time on the lake that day, although Eric became tired and napped for a while on the floor of the boat. Later, when we got home, Eric mowed the lawn for his dad. He had a habit of mowing funny designs and, that day, he mowed two smiley faces into the grass.

Picture of Eric taken by Katherine around this time

The next day—Sunday, September 13—was also beautiful, but on this day, Eric was feeling down. He didn't want to eat the breakfast I had made and ate potato chips instead. Afterward, we went to Mass and as we were leaving the church, I was walking behind Eric and Mike and noticed how tall Eric had grown. "Soon, he'll be taller than Mike!" I thought. Later that day, Eric needed to get his laundry and homework done, but his energy level was low and he seemed to be procrastinating throughout the day. On top of that, he had missed school on Tuesday of that week due to a migraine, so his workload was extra heavy. Nevertheless, Mike had planned for he and Eric to go to a friend's house that evening to trap shoot; it would be a fun activity for the two of them.

I made a nice meal for us that afternoon. Katherine had a friend over and we shared baked ham; a tomato, cucumber and onion salad; watermelon slices; and a pineapple upside-down cake—all Eric's favorites, especially watermelon. Once when he was little, Eric even asked if his birthday gift could be a big watermelon that he could eat all by himself! We had dinner at about 3 o'clock and then relaxed as Eric did his homework and laundry. At about 4 o'clock, we reminded him that he needed to be ready to go with Dad to trap shoot, but he said he had too much homework. He had been working on it off and on all afternoon, but still had a lot to do, and when it was time to go, he didn't feel like he should; he said he had to stay home and get his work done. So, we decided that I would go in his place. Eric offered me his yellow eye protector goggles that he wore when he and Nathan played paint ball or air soft wars. Then, just as we were getting ready to leave, I found Eric chatting with a friend on Facebook.

"I thought you had to do homework?" I said.

"I do," he replied. "I'm just taking a little break."

"If the reason you can't go with Dad is because of your homework, you need to get off Facebook and get busy getting it done," I replied.

I went to help Mike get ready and when I checked in on Eric again, he was preparing to sit down in our living room with his earphones in his ears, a spoon, and a bucket of ice cream in his hands. I surprised him and my anger erupted.

I started yelling at him and said, "How can we trust you, when this is what you do? Besides, we just ate dinner. You can't be hungry already!"

I grabbed the spoon and bucket of ice cream and told him to get to his homework.

Then, I went outside and told Mike what had happened.

"Tell him to come with us," he said.

So, I went in and found Eric in his bedroom on his bed with homework all around him.

"Eric, we want you to come with us," I said.

He gave me an exasperated look and lifted his sheets of homework.

"I can't!" he replied. "I have this and this and this to do!"

"Fine then," I said. "I expect to see what you've accomplished when we return."

So, we went to Mike's friend's house and Mike shot trap with him and his son. We had a nice visit, and when we got home, we went in to see how Eric was getting along with his homework. Katherine had just arrived home from shopping with her friend. Mike arrived at Eric's bedroom first and, finding him lying on his bedroom floor, he thought he was sleeping (Eric often had difficulty sleeping and would try to sleep in different places in our house, so this wasn't unusual for him). Then, when Katherine and I joined Mike, we all looked into Eric's bedroom and saw him lying on the floor. It wasn't until Katherine and I started screaming that Mike realized anything was wrong. While we won't share the painful details of the scene that met us, the horror we felt is indescribable and permanently etched in our memories. During the time that we had been gone, Eric had ended his life. As Mike and Katherine left Eric's room, I knelt down beside him, trying to make sense of this unimaginable tragedy. I realized that our lives were now torn in two; there would always be the dividing line of before this moment and after. Suddenly, I began to sense a loving presence and I felt as though I was being wrapped in love. When I touched Eric's hand, it felt cool.

"He's gone," I said as Mike came back into the room.

We left Eric's room and went upstairs to call 911. I called our dear friend Jan and my mom so they could alert family and friends of the tragedy and our need for prayer. An ambulance arrived and the EMT entered our home, went to Eric's room, and quickly left again. There was nothing anyone could do to help him. My mind was reeling. "He's left us. Our lives will never be the same. How could this have happened? Eric never said anything to any of us about wanting to do something like this. We would never have imagined that he would take his own life. How can we go on without him? Why hadn't my last words to him been, 'I love you, Eric!'" A police officer arrived and went downstairs by Eric, while Mike, Katherine, and I were upstairs together.

"We are not going to let this weaken our family," Mike said. "We will use this to strengthen our family and our faith."

Mike went with a police officer and picked Nathan up from his college in our town and broke the news to him. When they came home, we left our house together to go down to the chapel at our church. While we were gone, Eric's body was removed from our home. Jan had shared the news with our church family and many of them gathered to be with us in the chapel of our church. We arrived at the chapel at about 7:45 p.m. and Vicki, the church bookkeeper, came out to meet us. She embraced me as I slumped to my knees on the sidewalk outside the church.

Hugging me, she looked into my eyes, and said, "I understand."

As impossible as it seemed, I knew that somehow, she did. Later, we would learn that Vicki had experienced the death of a brother; she understood the depth of our devastation because she had witnessed the pain of her parents when her brother died.

. . .

The chapel at St. Thomas More is beautiful. We sat in the front pew, directly before the tabernacle that contains the consecrated hosts—our Lord Jesus, present in body, blood, soul, and divinity. I wanted to be as close to Jesus as physically possible. Meanwhile, such a large number of people had come to pray for us that many had no place to sit. What an immense comfort it was to hear the voices of our friends praying all around us; we felt wrapped in love and strengthened by their prayers. Our friends Todd and Royanna Stratmoen invited us to stay at their home, and we left the chapel at around 11:30 p.m. that night, but Mike and I didn't sleep. We just held each other and cried.

CHAPTER 8

"I have the strength for everything through him who strengthens me."
(Philippians 4:13)

Laura

The next morning, the image of Eric as we had found him kept invading my thoughts, and I suddenly heard in my mind the words, "See him in life! See him in life!" In unspeakable pain, we sought comfort in God's Word. We closed our eyes, prayed, and began allowing the Bible to fall open to random places. In the past, we had often found comfort and guidance in the Living Word of God in this way, and we believed He would help us now in our darkest hour. The first reading the Lord provided for us was Matthew 18:10-11:

"See that you do not despise one of these little ones, for I say to you that their angels in heaven always look upon the face of my heavenly Father."

I closed the Bible. Oh, dear God! With eyes closed and again allowing the pages to fall open, my eyes fell on the continuation of this reading—the very next word after the previous sentence that I had just read! I didn't realize this at the time, but I later discovered that I had interrupted the thought the Lord had wanted to share… so He picked it right up where He'd left off with Matthew 18:12-14:

"What is your opinion? If a man has a hundred sheep and one of them goes astray, will he not leave the ninety-nine in the hills and go in search of the stray?

And if he finds it, amen, I say to you, he rejoices more over it than over the ninety-nine that did not stray. In just the same way, it is not the will of your heavenly Father that one of these little ones be lost."

I repeated that last line in my mind, "It is not the will of your heavenly Father that one of these little ones be lost." I believed deep in my heart that this was God telling us that our precious Eric was not lost!

Our heavenly Father did not want him to be lost. Jesus had gone out to find him and bring him home to the place God had prepared for Eric in heaven. All I could think was, "Thank you, Eternal Father God! Thank you, Lord Jesus!"

For a third time, we allowed the Bible to fall open. This time, it opened to John 11:1-25, when Jesus was on his way to raise his friend Lazarus from the dead. On the way, He met Lazarus' sister, Martha. The dialogue between Martha and Jesus in verses 21-25 stood out for us:

*"Martha said to him, 'Lord, if you had been here, my brother would not have died.'… Jesus told her, 'Your brother will rise again.'
Martha said to him, 'I know he will rise, in the resurrection on the last day.'
Jesus told her, 'I am the Resurrection and the Life; whoever believes in me, even if he dies, will live, and everyone who lives and believes in me will never die.'"*

Eric believed in Jesus. He had even received our Lord in Holy Eucharist on the day he died. Oh God, you are so good! You gave us exactly the words we needed to hear in that moment to sustain us and help us focus on the eternal existence of our youngest son.

Then, we decided to pray the Rosary, and chose to pray the glorious mysteries: Jesus' Resurrection; His ascension into heaven; Jesus pours out his Holy Spirit on Blessed Mother Mary and the Apostles in the upper room at Pentecost; Jesus assumes Mary into heaven, body and soul, at the end of her earthly life; and Jesus crowns Mary queen of heaven and earth. As we prayed the Hail Mary prayers of the Rosary, I kept hearing the words, "He is with me! He is with me!" and I knew that Eric was with Our Blessed Mother in heaven.

Later that Monday morning, we went back to our parish chapel in the hopes of finding comfort, and church staff members and friends who were there came to us and prayed with and for us. Father Andrew Dickenson, the priest of the Newman Center on the SDSU campus, also met us there. He sat with us in the chapel and gave us hope in his presence and thoughtful words. He even said a Mass for our family and the few people who were present. It was such a comfort to us to receive our Lord Jesus in Holy Eucharist. Later that day, Father Andrew also came to our home and blessed Eric's bedroom and the rest of our house. That, too, was a great comfort.

We can't emphasize enough how important it is to reach out to those who are grieving. From the moment that Eric died, we were supported and lifted up by the loving actions and prayers of countless people. We will never be able to effectively express the thankfulness we feel toward everyone who reached out to us in love and supported us! However, a word of caution: ***Please be careful what you say to grieving people.*** Some people said things to us that were hurtful, and words spoken thoughtlessly can add to the griever's heartache. So, go, be present for the grievers, say how sorry you are for their loss, reach out with some meaningful gesture, and pray for their consolation and healing.

Many friends, as well as people from our family, church, workplaces, and the community, reached out to us to fill any needs we might have; we were cradled in the loving arms of these beautiful people and we were truly blessed to experience the presence of Christ in his mystical body, the Church. We were in shock, yet moving through the necessary motions, making preparations for Eric's funeral.

After staying a couple of nights at the Stratmoens' house, we wanted to return to our home. We never believed that Eric's spirit was lingering in our house; rather, we knew that he went to the Lord and is now in His loving arms. And, while it felt good to be alone together as a family, it was incredibly painful to be without Eric.

On Wednesday morning, Father Rod Farke, the pastor of our parish, came to our house to help us plan the liturgy for the funeral. As we spoke, he seemed to sense our deep emotional torment and offered to privately hear our confessions, which was another incredible blessing. Feelings of guilt are one of the most difficult aspects of losing a loved one to suicide. And, as Eric's parents, Mike and I felt an immense burden of guilt for what we believed we should or should not have done that might have prevented Eric's final act.

After my confession, Father Rod asked me, "Do you believe in Jesus?"

"Yes, I do," I replied.

"Do you believe that He died on the cross for you?" he asked.

"Yes, I do!" I said.

"Then, you must leave this guilt at the foot of His cross," he said. "Accept the forgiveness He has already given you. You know, Satan will try to use this tragedy to destroy your family. You cannot allow him to do that!"

These words would return to my mind many times in the future.

. . .

On Thursday morning, I awoke very early, around 4 o'clock. I went into the dining room and looked at the pictures we had spread across the table as we were in the process of choosing pictures of Eric to display at his wake and funeral. After a while, I went back to bed, and when I woke back up at 7:15, I decided to call some friends to see if they would go and pray with me in the chapel. When I called one friend, I reached her husband, who reminded me that there was a 7 o'clock morning Mass on Thursdays—I had completely forgotten although I usually attended that Mass. I thought, "Oh well. I'll just drive down to the chapel and pray a while with my friends after Mass is finished." However, when I opened the garage door to leave, my car was blocked by the cars of those who were staying with us. So, I decided to walk to church, which was only about 15 minutes away. On the way, I met a girl out walking her dog, a beagle. We had seen this little girl on many occasions, ever since the dog was a puppy, which Eric had loved because beagles were always his favorite breed. As the girl and her dog approached me, I greeted them and stooped down to pet the dog. I learned his name was Oscar; he was so wiggly and full of life. For several moments, as I petted him, he sat still and looked into my eyes. Then, he was all wiggles and squirmy puppy body again. I laughed and thanked the girl for letting me visit them. As they went on their way, I had a feeling that this moment was a gift from Eric. It was as if he were saying, "I'm okay, Mom. I love you!" In that moment, I realized that if I had remembered there was Mass this morning, and if I hadn't been blocked in and unable to drive, I would have missed out on this gift. I thanked God for this blessing.

Mike

When Laura left for church, I got out of bed and went to get a cup of coffee. However, as I walked past our dining room table to look out the patio doors, I noticed something sitting on one of the chairs by the table. It was a leaf that had been given to us by the priest in Wisconsin who had helped me discern whether I should leave my business. I left it where it was, wondering how it had gotten there. That morning, I was extremely sad, missing Eric terribly; I just kept crying and went to sit on the front stoop of our home. I was still sitting there when Laura returned, and she excitedly shared the sign she had received from Eric.

The leaf Mike found on the chair

After she told me about Oscar the beagle, I said, "I'm glad you got that sign, Laura, but I need a sign of my own."

When we went back inside the house, I pointed to the leaf on the chair by the table and asked Laura if she knew where it had come from.

After looking at it, she turned to me and said, "Mike, there's your sign!"

The leaf was sitting perfectly in the center of the chair and pointing directly at Eric's pictures on the table. Hand-painted on the surface of the delicate leaf is an image of Jesus after his resurrection, The Risen Lord!

"Mike, that's the chair I was sitting on at 4 o'clock this morning," Laura said. "That leaf wasn't there then! Look at it. It's the Risen Lord, and it's pointing toward the pictures of Eric on the table! The message is Eric is with the Risen Lord, WHO CONQUERED SIN AND DEATH!"

We wondered how the leaf could have gotten there. Normally, we kept it tucked away safely within the pages of our family Bible because it was hand-painted in India and is very fragile. But the Bible was on top of a buffet cabinet next to the dining room table, whereas the chair where we found the leaf was on the opposite side of the dining room table. But, although Laura was thrilled by this beautiful sign, I was left wanting more.

Laura

Royanna's work on the picture signboards was another amazing gift. With these and some of Eric's most prized possessions—like his electric guitar and bicycle—we created a beautiful display of the joy our family had shared during Eric's lifetime. One of the items in the display was a book of poetry that Eric had written for a school project. His poems are a window into his personality and his amazing sense of humor, as well as his deep pain and sadness. Following is a sample of the poems Eric wrote in this book. Any grammatical or other errors occur as he wrote them:

Things to do

I hate poetry, the way it rhymes; it's a waste of time.

In fact, I'd rather
Hunt for mountain lions with a pocket knife,
Skydive with a lead parachute,
Fish for piranhas with my toes,
Give myself open heart surgery with a rusty pair of pliers,
Walk into a war zone with a squirt gun,
Cut down a redwood tree with a nail file,
J-walk through the auto bon,
Walk barefoot through a razor blade factory,
Fly a kite in an electrical plant,
Take a walk in a bomb test site.
All of these I would rather do than write poetry.

Eric

Smart, tall, cool, calm,
Friend of Vlad, Dane,
Lover of democracy, Christianity, girls,
Who felt sad, mad, confused,
Who needed friends, family, music,
Who gave knowledge, help, friendship,
Who feared Barney, puppets, loss,
Who would have liked to see peace, GH championship,
The battle of Shiloh,
Resident of Brookings, SD
Kondratuk

Old Acoustic

I live in your closet.
I can see your old books.
I can taste all the dust.
I have two broken strings.

I'm your old acoustic.
I remember how you played me all the time.
I was afraid to be replaced.
Now I dream of being played again.
I hear you play that electric.
I don't understand why you prefer him.
My name is the old forgotten acoustic.

Freedom

Freedom is blue of the open night sky.
It smells like pine needles and cut grass;
it tastes like stew cooked over an open fire.
It sounds like chains falling to the ground.
It feels like running with no reason to go back.
It looks like an open turf with no obstacles in my way.
Freedom is a bird.

Life

Life is my fingers, moving across the strings.
Life is my sword, with which I play.
Life is my pencil with which I write notes.
Life is my songs, with which I express myself.

Eric had a fantastic talent for playing guitar and had begun to write music. So, our nephew, Jake, put together a video that included pictures of Eric and a recording of him playing his own music that looped on a large screen and made it feel as though Eric was right there with us.

Sometime after the funeral, our friend Laura told us that when she watched the video, she heard a young man's voice singing words to the song Eric played. However, the music recording only includes different tracks of Eric playing his guitar; there aren't any vocal parts. But we later discovered that Eric had actually written words to this song—which he entitled "Asleep"—and Laura said the young man she heard singing had sounded happy.

Mike

Eric's wake was on Thursday, September 17. Before everyone came to share their condolences, I wanted our immediate family to have time alone with Eric and our thoughts. I was an emotional wreck, crying uncontrollably; the pain was so deep and I couldn't find comfort. In fact, I think Father Rod and the church staff were concerned that I might not make it through the evening. Plus, looking at the display of photos and Eric's favorite possessions, as well as hearing him play his guitar on the video, made the pain even more intense. So, when I saw Eric's casket in the church sanctuary, I decided to go down to it and pray. Looking at his picture sitting atop the closed casket, I knelt down and placed my hand on his wooden casket above his head and began to pray. As I did, I heard Eric speak to me and had a memory all at the same time. The memory was the first Christmas after Eric learned that Santa wasn't real. After opening his gifts, he seemed disappointed. Although he said he liked his gifts, he seemed down. When I asked why, he replied that he was sad that he hadn't received everything on his wish list that he had given us. It was true; I always replaced one of the gifts our children wanted with a surprise gift to help teach them that they should be happy with whatever they receive.

"Eric, don't be sad for what you didn't get; be happy for what you did receive," I remember saying to him.

And, at that moment, I heard Eric's voice saying, "Dad, don't be sad for the time we didn't have; be happy for the time we had!"

I realized that Eric was giving me my own lesson. These words and the simultaneous memory filled me with the strength I needed to get up and face the wake, the funeral, and the rest of the day and evening.

Laura

Father Rod did a wonderful job with his message that night, as well as his homily at the funeral the next day. His words, the readings we chose, and the songs that were so beautifully sung by the church and high school choirs gave us great comfort.

Father Rod's words on Thursday evening especially touched and comforted our broken hearts:

> *To the Kondratuk family, I know I speak for everyone here as we offer our prayers, sympathy, and support to you in a terribly difficult time, perhaps the worst in your lives. We gather tonight and tomorrow to pay our respects to Eric, to remember all he meant to us, and give thanks for that, and to pray to the Most Merciful God to receive Eric into eternal life and peace, with his depression and discouragement left far behind. We are also gathering to pray for and support you, Eric's family, as you endure this horrible suffering.*
>
> *"Our gospel reading beginning in desolation, ends in hope: Mary and Martha's brother, Lazarus, has died, and Martha complains to Jesus, 'If you had been here, my brother would not have died.' Yet, she has hope: 'But, even now, I know that whatever you ask of God, God will give you.' Then, Jesus reassures Martha, as He reassures you,*

Laura and Mike, Nathan and Katherine, 'I am the resurrection and the life; whoever believes in me, even if he dies, will live, and everyone who lives and believes in me will never die.'

'Then He asks Martha, and He also asks you and me, 'Do you believe this?'

'May these funeral liturgies, and may all the loving support that has been given and received during these days, help all of us to believe this—that Jesus' love for Eric has not come to an end, and Eric, though he has died, is living, with the Lord, in a glorified body in the Kingdom of Heaven." [1]

We are so thankful to Father Rod for these hope-filled, thoughtful and compassionate words!

Eric's guitar teacher, as well as his seventh and eighth grade teachers, also shared their thoughts about him. The following words were written and shared by Karen Thaler, Eric's seventh grade homeroom teacher.

Dear Eric,

We are broken-hearted at the middle school. When we stop crying, honestly, we've been angry at you. At times, we've wanted to shake you and yell, "What were you thinking?" And then, we realize you weren't thinking. You were just feeling. The boy we know and love would not intentionally hurt others or cause such devastating pain.

And that's the boy we remember today and the one we will remember forever. The boy who lived. The boy who cared for others. The boy who made a new student feel welcome to our school by helping her open her locker and always being kind to her.

The boy with such a sense of humor. The kind of humor that doesn't yell out, "Look at me," but the kind of humor that's subtle and quiet and is even funnier as we remember it. (Like hiding dollar bills in books throughout the homeroom for classmates and teacher to find). The boy who we see at registration with his mom and we say, "Eric, you can come back to our grade and do it over" AND we mean it! We remember the boy who had such a strong work ethic, and such strong values. Honest and dependable. We remember a boy we were proud to call our own.[2]

Then, a very sensitive gesture was offered. The mourners were invited to take a piece of paper and write a memory or thought of Eric for his family to read later. Once they had completed their message, they brought their papers forward and placed them into a basket in front of the altar. At the same time, they lit a votive candle and placed it in front of the altar, as well. When they were all finished, there was a long line of glowing, colored candles. It made me think of how our light shines in the darkness, and that it continues to shine even after we leave this life and go on to eternal life. We treasure those pieces of paper with thoughts of Eric from his friends, schoolmates and family members.

Here is one example of those meaningful notes:

Dear Kondratuk Family,

I knew Eric in 6th grade, 7th grade, 8th grade, and, of course, ... various things from the church. I was new in Mickelson Middle School, and your son one day just came right up to me and didn't ask me where I was from, why I was here, or any "newcomer" questions. Eric talked to me like he knew me my entire life, and that meant the world to me. We went on through the couple of years we knew each other as friends. We ended up in the same CCD class and realized how we were both extremely conservative and pro-life. Eric made me cards with funny phrases or Republican jokes. My favorite one was pro-life and it said, "A person's a person no matter how small." – Dr. Seuss. For the short time I knew your dear son, I wouldn't have changed for the world. I just wish they were longer. He showed me to turn to God in all my struggles. I really believe that boy has changed my life. Eric lived his life the way we all should. I can't tell you how truly sorry I am, but right now, Eric is playing his beautiful music for the angels. You couldn't have loved that boy better. I don't know why this happened, perhaps we will never know, but I know one thing…that card Eric gave me will be in my pocket for the rest of my life. And whoever asks, "Who did that?" I'll simply reply, "An angel."

– R.N. (13 years old, 8th grade)

Mike

After the wake, I was talking with John Meilahn, our friend from my second pilgrimage to Medjugorje. During this conversation, we discovered something amazing. On Tuesday of this terrible week—at the same moment in the day—we both looked to the Bible for words of comfort, and the reading we both received was Matthew 5:3-11. We realized that this reading spoke to us about Eric, his character, and the reward he was now receiving in heaven.

> *"Blessed are the poor in spirit, for theirs is the kingdom of heaven.*
> *Blessed are they who mourn, for they will be comforted.*

Blessed are the meek, for they will inherit the land.
Blessed are they who hunger and thirst for justice, they will
be satisfied.
Blessed are the merciful, for they will be shown mercy.
Blessed are the clean of heart, for they will see God.
Blessed are the peacemakers, for they will be called children
of God.
Blessed are they who are persecuted for the sake of
righteousness, for theirs is the kingdom of heaven.
Blessed are you when they insult you and persecute you and
utter every kind of evil against you (falsely) because of me.
Rejoice and be glad, for your reward will be great in heaven.
Thus they persecuted the prophets who were before you."

We took out a Bible and read through these verses and realized that this reading describes Eric! He stood up to bullies who put him down for his strong beliefs. He was meek, pure of heart, and humble. He tried to be a peacemaker. He hungered for justice and would take others under his wing, especially those who were seen as different. (In fact, we had thought Eric would make a good policeman when he grew up because of his strong sense of right and wrong.) He was even persecuted for the sake of righteousness; what we didn't know until after he was gone was that Eric had been a victim of bullying. But now, he was experiencing his great reward—the place Jesus had prepared for him in the Heavenly Kingdom.

Laura

Friday, September 18, 2009, dawned bright and beautiful; it was the day we would lay the body of our youngest child to rest. We were amazed at the number of people who made a special effort to be there for us, especially those from Wisconsin who drove six hours and returned home the same day! Every time we turned around, another friend or family member was there to reach out and hug us or share a thought about Eric. We were so very blessed by these beautiful people; we can't express the depth of our gratitude for their kindness.

Before the funeral began, we gathered into the little chapel that had been such a source of comfort to us in the last few days and began to pray the Rosary. As we did so, a vision formed in my mind. I saw four tiny trees growing in a desolate place. A powerful wind was blowing them over, and I sensed that they would soon be ripped from the ground. Then, the weak little saplings began to reach out and entwine their branches with each other. They grew together in their combined state and became strong, tall, thick, and immovable. And, although the wind still howled, it didn't affect the trees at all. I realized that this was our family! We needed to stand together to weather this life storm.

The day before, I had decided to write down our family thoughts and memories of Eric to be shared at his funeral Mass, and a dear friend from Wisconsin had agreed to read it for us. He did a beautiful job of speaking these words for us that we were unable say for ourselves:

Thoughts from Eric's Family

Eric had a little boy's spirit in a grown man's body. At just 14 years old, he stood six foot tall and showed no sign of stopping. Within this ever-growing young man was a very sensitive, pure, generous heart. Eric loved little children; he had a soft spot for them and they were drawn to him. He always cracked a smile when he saw little kids.

Eric was very curious. He would see something interesting and take off running to explore and savor it. This was a bit of a problem when he was little, as we were always asking, "Where's Eric?" His curiosity led him to be very imaginative and inventive.

From the time he was little, he loved to collect materials that he could incorporate into what he called his "contraptions." He collected and built with Legos, wood, plastic, cardboard tubes, and boxes; anything and everything could play into his imagination and be useful.

He would ask, "Can I have that? I can make something with it." This included him searching through refuse bins on construction sites. (We had to tell him to stop that.) Eric would often gift family and friends with his creations. His favorite words even as a very little boy were, "I have an idea!" And, boy, did he ever!

Eric's generosity showed in the way he gave flowers to Mommy and gifted Daddy with handmade treasures and Nathan with CDs of his original music. For Katherine, he came into her room at night and softly played his guitar to help her go to sleep, and he'd helped her practice her lines for a musical audition. These are just a few of the countless ways he showed us his love.

He saw the world and appreciated the beauty in God's creation to the smallest detail. Eric liked to point out and share his discoveries. He loved to pick up special rocks and pebbles. We often came home from a vacation with bags of rocks, shells, or petrified wood that he just couldn't part with. Last Saturday morning, he was busy at the shore of Lake Poinsett collecting tiny pebbles he fancied and picking flowers for Mom.

Eric was a born leader and teacher. He liked to think about how a thing could be done and then teach others his discovery. He had a great sense of humor and liked to gain the title, "class clown." He could make us laugh with the simplest comment. Then, Nathan would say, "Good one, Boo Boo!" Eric enjoyed listening to comedians such as Brian Regen, Jerry Seinfeld, Uncle Dan, and Uncle Don.

His joy in life was playing guitar and, in the last year, his ability developed amazingly. He was deeply passionate about his beliefs and would stand up for them in the face of ridicule. Faith in God our Father, Jesus Christ our Lord, the Holy Spirit, and Our Blessed Mother was the foundation in his life.

We thank you, Lord God, for the unique, beautiful, precious gift of our Eric. In his young life, he touched so many and taught us how to love. Hold him tenderly, close to your heart, Lord Jesus. Please lead him home into your loving embrace. Fill him with everlasting peace, love, and life. May he experience the joy of your presence until we meet again.

We love you, Eric Walter!

Dad, Mom, Nathan, and Katherine

Many people commented to us after the wake and funeral services that they admired our grace and strength throughout these sad days, but it was our deep faith in God the Father, the Lord Jesus, His gift of salvation and promise of eternal life, and the signs He was supplying for us that Eric was with Him that helped sustain us in those most difficult days. The actions and prayers of the many, many people who lifted us up in our darkest hours enabled us to continue putting one foot in front of the other and walk into our future without Eric Walter.

CHAPTER 9

Laura

After Eric's funeral, we continued to be surprised by the ways the Lord was reaching out to us with gifts of comfort and strength. For instance, the next morning, Katherine was looking at the pictures of Eric that were still spread out on the dining room table when she noticed one picture showing our friend Kevin with Nathan and Eric. The picture had been taken at Nathan's confirmation, and Eric was standing between them, holding a framed painting we had given to Kevin for being Nathan's confirmation sponsor.

"Look at the picture Eric is holding!" Katherine said.

In that painting, Jesus is embracing a young man as he enters heaven. This image would be used by the Lord again and again to reinforce for us the place that Eric now calls home.

That day, as well, Mike's brother John shared with us that earlier in the week he had had two dreams about Eric. In the first dream, he saw Eric at his final age. He was sitting bent over with his head in his hands, regretting what he had done and the fact that he couldn't take it back; he hadn't realized how much his action would hurt us. John said that he believed this dream meant that Eric was asking for our forgiveness for what he had done. Then, in the second dream, John saw a couple walking toward him with a little boy between them holding their hands. As they came closer, John recognized that the couple was his parents, Wladimir and Magdalena Kondratuk—both of whom had died many years ago—and the little boy was Eric at around three or four years old. Eric looked up at his grandparents and smiled, then the three of them turned around and walked away together. What a comforting image this was for all of us.

Later that day, we opened a gift that our friend Sally had given us, a painting on clay of Jesus the Good Shepherd holding a little lamb. Sally always included prayer cards with her gifts, and when we looked at the one she had given us, we were shocked—it was the same painting that we had given Kevin and that Katherine had noticed Eric holding in the picture! However, on Sally's prayer card, the young man that Jesus is embracing as he enters heaven looks exactly like Eric, with the same shape head and sandy blond hair. We learned that the painting is called, "The Homecoming," and the prayer on the back reads, "O Blessed Trinity, Father, Son and Holy Spirit, embrace me in my spiritual needs, now and at the time of my death."

After the funeral, our extended family returned home and we were left alone. And, although our church friends came with meals for us for several weeks and various friends stopped in periodically to visit and show their support, it was time for us to move into our "new normal." The house was quiet and lonely, and we all missed hearing Eric practice his guitar, as well as his constant chatter when we were trying to watch TV, and his silly jokes and one-liners that cracked us up. The space that one person occupies in the hearts of those who love him is immense.

One morning, a couple of weeks after Eric died, I was praying in his room. Feeling miserable, I wanted to find comfort in the Word of God, so I allowed the pages of my Bible to fall open and was surprised to read these words:

"Woe to those who tug at guilt with cords of perversity." (Isaiah 5:18)

This wasn't exactly what I had hoped for; I felt the Lord gently scolding me for remaining steeped in the feelings of guilt that kept beating me down. I also recalled what Father Rod had said to me after my confession, and I knew that I needed to leave my guilt at the foot of the cross because Jesus had already forgiven me. But that was easier said than done; the "whys," "if onlys," and "what ifs" constantly inundated my thoughts. Irrational as it was, I seemed to be desperately trying to find a way to change the outcome; if only I could discover answers to the questions that ran on an endless loop through my mind.

I had always taken pride in my parenting skills and enjoyed the compliments we received on our children's good behavior and grades in school; I loved visiting with teachers at parent-teacher conferences and hearing them make comments like, "I wish I could be a fly on the wall in your home because you are doing everything right!" But now, in addition to losing our precious child and our dreams for his future, I had also lost my sense of self-worth. I had believed I was a good parent, so how could this have happened? I thought, "What kind of mother must I be to not have responded appropriately to Eric's needs, to not have seen this coming, to not have done everything in my power to prevent it?" I kept hearing the word "FAILURE" pounding incessantly in my mind. "You are a *failure* at being a mother! You *failed* to be there for Eric when he needed you most! Your life's work is a *failure!*" My self-recriminations were endless, and my self-hatred was growing.

So, in an effort to find healing and peace, Mike and I joined various grief support groups. We attended the first one just a few weeks after Eric died. It was for general grief after the death of a loved one. The second was to learn how to grieve through the holidays. Third—and most helpful for me—was specific to those grieving a suicide loss. In attending these grief support groups, we learned that grieving is a process. It takes time to move through the grief journey, and no two people grieve in exactly the same way. Moreover, depending on the manner of death and the relationship with the person who died, it can take a very long time to heal. The fact that Eric died by suicide and that we found him would make the journey toward healing even more challenging for us. Additionally, we learned that, although there are recognizable stages in the grieving process, these stages don't happen in a precise order. Rather, they occur randomly and unpredictably; each person has their own journey to walk toward the acceptance of the death of a loved one, and no one can instruct someone else on how to do this. However, people can use coping strategies and receive support as they find their way through their personal journeys of bereavement.

Additionally, for some time after Eric's death, I suffered from post-traumatic stress. I was afraid to open closed doors in our home—fearful of what I might find on the other side—and a feeling of panic would rise up within me if I didn't receive a response when I called Mike, Nathan, or Katherine. What's more, for months after Eric's death—and without warning—I would periodically see the wound he had inflicted upon himself superimposed on other children. I always felt a jolt of horror when this occurred, and I'd try to take a deep breath to regain my emotional balance. In some of these moments, I would go to a private place and just let the tears flow. I'd pray, "Help me, Jesus! Please help me! Give me strength!"

Meanwhile, I also struggled in my job at the library because so many book covers depict graphic violence. In fact, several times per day, I would be shocked by a violent image that took me right back to Eric's side on the night he died, seeing him as we found him. This was especially jarring because I never knew when I might see such an image; there was no opportunity to prepare myself or look away, and the shock was always terrible. I felt as though I would take two steps forward in my grief journey and then suddenly be forced three steps back. As a result, I eventually made the difficult decision to leave that job. Although my coworkers were wonderful friends and I really liked the work, I had to protect myself from seeing those upsetting images.

. . .

Mike, Katherine, and I sought professional counseling, and it helped to talk with someone who made us feel comfortable and was nonjudgmental. Our counselor helped us understand that the feelings, thoughts, and emotions we were suffering were normal for anyone who had survived the trauma we had experienced. Nonetheless, at times, the pain was so great that I wished I could just die myself and join Eric in heaven; Mike said he felt that way at times, too. And, while I knew I would never take my own life, I thought that if I got sick, I just wouldn't try to fight to stay here. However, Mike, Nathan, and Katherine reminded me that we needed one another and that we had to go on and live for each other.

Part III

CHAPTER 10

Laura

Before Eric died, I had scheduled my second pilgrimage to Medjugorje. I had been excited about the idea and couldn't wait to get back to that holy place. But now, I felt as though I couldn't leave my family when they needed me and I needed them.

"Laura, you have to go," Mike said. "Don't you know, any graces you receive will not just be for you? They'll be for all of us. We need all the graces we can get right now!"

So, just six weeks after Eric's death, I found myself back in Medjugorje with Julie Hopkins, the wife of Mike's lifelong friend Don. Julie and I had been friends for many years, and when she decided that she also wanted to make a pilgrimage to Medjugorje, we were able to experience this trip together.

. . .

Our Blessed Mother, the Virgin Mary, reached out to Mike personally to help him achieve a life-changing conversion back to her Son, Jesus. But that's only part of Mary's story in Medjugorje. Here's how it all started:

On the evening of June 24, 1981, Ivanka Ivankovic, 15, and her friend, Mirjana Dragicevic, 16, were talking together as they walked along the dirt road that wove its way from the village of Bijakovici along the base of the hill called Podbrodo. They sat down to rest when Ivanka suddenly noticed the shining figure of a woman up on the hill.

She exclaimed to Mirjana, "I think I see Our Lady on the hill!"

"Yeah, sure it's Our Lady!" Mirjana replied. "She came to see what the two of us are up to because she has nothing better to do."

Ivanka continued to insist that she was seeing the Blessed Mother. Mirjana at first left in anger but, feeling that something was calling her back, returned to find Ivanka jumping up and down.

Ivanka begged Mirjana, "Look now, please!"

Mirjana slowly turned and looked up at the hill. She had a hard time processing what she saw...a beautiful young woman in a bluish-grey dress holding an infant.

A boy named Ivan Dragicevic came by carrying apples. When he saw what they saw, he dropped the apples and ran away.

Their friend, Vicka Ivankovic, 17, found them there.

"Look up there," they said, but when Vicka learned they were seeing Gospa (the Croatian word for the Blessed Mother), she became frightened and ran away. Then, Ivanka and Mirjana looked at each other and without a word ran to their homes.

The next day, the children felt drawn to return to the spot. Mirjana,

Ivanka, Vicka, Ivan, and two others who were not with them on the first day, Marija Pavlovic, 16 years old, and her cousin, 10-year-old Jakov Colo, joined the group at Vicka's request. All were amazed to see the same figure they'd seen the day before up on the hill. [1]

Time has passed and the six visionaries are now adults who have chosen to have families.

Blessed Mother Mary's main message is peace. She desires for all people to turn to Jesus her Son and to love one another. There are five tasks Our Blessed Mother Mary asks everyone to undertake: read the Bible, attend Mass, experience the sacrament of reconciliation once a month, fast on bread and water on Wednesdays and Fridays for the conversion of sinners and the salvation of souls, and to pray from the heart (especially the Rosary) daily.

. . .

My second pilgrimage took place from October 26 to November 4, 2009. On the night we arrived in Medjugorje, Julie and I climbed Apparition Hill and prayed the Divine Mercy Chaplet together at the foot of the statue of Our Blessed Mother. It was a beautiful, starry night, and we could hear the people in St. James Church singing during the pilgrim's Mass. The sound of their voices gently wafted toward us on breezes from far below. It was so peaceful and, in that moment, we felt that this would be a very healing pilgrimage.

During our first few days in Medjugorje, we had several opportunities for deep prayer. We participated in the Masses, a healing Rosary led by Stephanie, and all of the prayer services offered at St. James Church. They were all very moving, and each offered the opportunity for deep fellowship with Jesus and Our Blessed Mother. Then, one day, as we prayed the Rosary at the time of the Apparition, I felt hands placed upon my head in blessing right before Mass. This was purely a sensation; there was not actually a person present doing this. I sensed that it was the Blessed Mother; I think she was giving me her motherly blessing because she knew I needed it, and it was an incredible moment filled with the Holy Spirit.

On Friday, October 30, 2009, our tour group was privileged to hear one of Father Svetozar Kralijevic's beautiful talks. Father Svetozar lived in Medjugorje and had been closely involved with the visionaries since the apparitions had begun. At the time of my pilgrimage, he ran an orphanage in Medjugorje, gave talks for pilgrims, and was a spiritual director. He had also written several books about Our Blessed Mother in Medjugorje and was a well-known figure in the history of the apparitions there. The lectures given by priests like Father Svetozar and visionaries often take place in a large yellow building behind St. James Church and are always packed with pilgrims, and this day was no exception. Afterward, I had an impulse to try and catch up to him through the crowd. I wanted to receive a blessing from him, if possible. As

Julie Hopkins and Laura outside St. James Church in Medjugorje[2]

I tried to hurry, I reached into my purse and took out my wallet with Eric's picture. I wanted to tell Father about Eric and ask him to pray for Eric's soul and for the healing of our family. When I finally reached him, he was out of the building and surrounded by a crowd of people.

"Father Svetozar," I said, touching his arm.

"Yes?" he replied, looking at me.

"Would you please pray for the soul of my son, Eric?" I asked. "He was 14 years old when he died by suicide on September 13— just six weeks ago."

Apparition Hill in the springtime with the statue of the Blessed Mother visible in the center toward the top of the hill

To my surprise, Father Svetozar reached out and hugged me, and I saw compassion and sadness in his eyes. Then, reaching into the pocket of his brown Franciscan priest's robe, he pulled out his wooden rosary and gently placed it upon Eric's picture in my hands.

"I will pray for you," he said.

I will always cherish this blessing.

The name Medjugorje means "between the mountains." True to its name, the village of Medjugorje is tucked between the hills and mountains that surround it. On one side of the village is Apparition Hill, where the Blessed Mother first appeared to the visionaries and where she has continued to appear to them many times since. A pilgrim can climb Apparition Hill while praying the mysteries of Rosary, which are now beautifully depicted in bronze sculptures on a lighted pathway. From a distance at night, it looks like a rosary of light laid out across the hillside.

On the other side of the village is Cross Mountain. Here, as well, Mary has appeared many times throughout the years to the visionaries, villagers, and pilgrims. The Stations of the Cross are portrayed beautifully in bronze along the rugged, mile-long pathway to the cross at the top, and the surfaces of the stone paths are worn smooth on both hillsides from the footsteps of millions of pilgrims who have crossed them.

Cross Mountain

Even before the apparitions began, the people of this area were very devout Catholics, and Mary told the visionaries that this is why she appears there. The people of Medjugorje have always clung to their faith in spite of persecution. In fact, in 1933, they built a cross atop Cross Mountain to commemorate the 1900th anniversary of Christ's crucifixion. The cross can be seen from miles around, and it's truly amazing that they were able to complete this project. They had to haul the cement and water up this mountain with a bucket brigade through brambles and over large, rough rocks. Just imagine these rugged people handing bucket after bucket of water and cement up a treacherous mountainside. It's inspiring to consider how much willpower and grit it must have taken to get the job done.

On the morning of Saturday, October 31, we climbed Cross Mountain. Stephanie told us to find a rock at the bottom that would represent our deepest pain or burden. Then, we would each carry that burden to the top of the mountain, place it at the foot of the cross, and leave it there. As I looked for the biggest rock I could carry, Father Rod's words echoed in my mind:

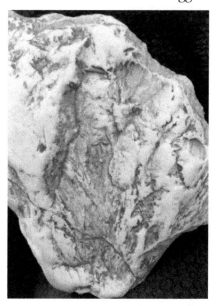

"You must leave this guilt at the foot of His cross. Accept the forgiveness He has already given you. You know, Satan will try to use this tragedy to destroy your family. You cannot allow him to do that!"

At the fourth station where Jesus meets His Mother, I was upset. I could imagine the pain Mary must have felt in her

The miracle rock

heart for her precious son, seeing Him tortured and suffering on His way to Calvary and not being able to prevent His pain or help Him. I felt intense pain for the loss of Eric and the suffering he had endured and I wept. Looking down, I checked to be sure that these tears were landing on the rock I held because I intended to leave them with the rock at the foot of the cross. I noticed that I was holding the rock with the opposite side up from the way I had originally picked it up. My tears were falling on the rock and it was wet. Sunlight shone over my shoulder onto the wet surface and I immediately noticed an image formed by the natural texture of the rock. As clearly as if it had been chiseled into the stone, I saw the image of Our Blessed Mother holding the infant Jesus. I could see her face, eyebrows, eyes, and nose, surrounded by her robe. I could see her right shoulder, and her right arm and hand were outstretched. The detail was so intricate that I could even make out the folds in the robe she was wearing. She appeared to be standing on a rocky surface, and above her head was a bird whose wings seemed to shoot out into the shape of flames. In the spot where her heart would be located, I could see a light-colored spot with dark flames radiating from it. And she held baby Jesus in her left arm bundled in a blanket with her left hand clasping Him. I could see His tiny right hand touching the side of His face, and above His head was a large halo. I must have had an astonished look on my face because the people around me took notice and gathered closer to see for themselves before gasping in amazement.

"Laura, you can't leave that here!" one woman said. "It's a sign! Blessed Mother is not just holding baby Jesus, she is also holding Eric for you!"

Needless to say, I didn't leave that rock on Cross Mountain. Instead, I picked up another one to represent my burden. After all, Mike had said that I was taking all of our family with me and that whatever blessings I received were for all of us, so I knew I needed to bring this image home for them to see, as well. Plus, Father Svetozar encouraged pilgrims to take rocks as a remembrance of their pilgrimage, rather than getting caught up in shopping for souvenirs. I believe that the Lord and Our Blessed Mother prepared that gift for our family and gave it to us as something solid to hold onto in the dark times when our pain is greatest. It was a way that we could see with our eyes and hold in our hands how to trust and be not afraid. To this day, I am so thankful for this incredible gift and the strength it gives me when I look at it and touch it. We share this gift with others, and those who are also able to see the image are moved with the wonder of this beautiful sign.

Laura showing Julie the miracle rock moments after discovering the image[3]

The next day was All Saint's Day, and we began it by walking to the blue cross at the base of Apparition Hill. With the influx of millions of pilgrims to Medjugorje over the years, vendors have built up little shop stands all over the village, even up to the foot of Apparition Hill and Cross Mountain. Winding through the vendor stands, we approached the blue cross, and on display in front of one of the gift stands, I noticed the painting called, "Home at Last," (the one of Jesus embracing a young man entering heaven) by Danny Hahlbohm. It was the beautiful sign that the Lord has shown us repeatedly to tell us that Eric is in heaven. I decided that, after our prayer time, I would purchase it to place in the prayer space we had created in Eric's old bedroom.

Later, Stephanie led us in a peace Rosary and, although it was a beautiful, cloudless day, I was feeling especially sad because this was the seven-week anniversary of Eric's death. However, after the Rosary, Julie and I walked to Mass and, amazingly, many of the readings spoke to me personally and comforted me. We heard, "I am the resurrection and the life. Whoever lives and believes in me will never die," and "Come unto me all you who are heavily burdened and I will give you rest." And, finally, the Beatitudes.

After dinner, we went back to church and stood in line to participate in the sacrament of Reconciliation. I went to a priest who prayed with me and said he would say a Mass for me that day. He also said I needed to let go of the thoughts that brought me down; I needed to move forward. But, afterward, I was extremely sad and didn't want to go into the packed church. So, I walked by the Risen Cross into the graveyard behind the church and prayed at the grave of Father Slavko Barbaric, a very holy priest who died on Cross Mountain. Then, after hearing the sounds of voices singing the opening song of the Mass, I decided to attend Mass in the outdoor altar space behind St. James Church. When Mass ended, I met a couple from our group, Frank and Connie, and walked with them to the votive candle area at the side of the church, where dozens of candles were burning. I saw a star shining directly over the head of Jesus on the large crucifix there and went into the church and joined everyone in praying the Glorious Mysteries of the Rosary. It was comforting to focus on Jesus' resurrection, His ascension into heaven, His pouring forth of His Holy Spirit, and the assumption and coronation of the Blessed Mother Mary—to focus on what Jesus has won for us by His life, death, and resurrection—namely, eternal life!

I walked back with a group from our tour and settled in the

dining hall, where Stephanie led us in a guided imagery prayer. We imagined ourselves walking down a long set of stairs to a heavy, wooden doorway. Then, we were to open the door into a beautiful garden. As I imagined opening that heavy door, I looked inside and, in this lush garden, I saw Eric standing behind a stone bench waiting for me. He had a bunch of flowers in his hands and gave them to me, and we were together when Jesus came into the garden. I ran to Jesus and hugged Him, and then the Blessed Mother came in and joined us. It was so beautiful to have that time with the three of them! I heard Stephanie instructing us to turn and leave the garden and go back out the door, but I didn't want to go!

"It's okay, Mom," Eric said. "I'll see you soon."

"Soon to you is not the same as soon to me, Eric," I thought. I was sad to have to leave, yet I had an immense feeling of peace after this experience, and I was very thankful that Stephanie had provided the opportunity for us to enter into prayer in this way. It was a healing experience that I really needed that day.

Monday, November 2, was All Souls Day, and it was a most amazing day! The graces that were poured out were unimaginable! We left at 6:30 a.m. to find a place to be present for Mirjana's monthly apparition at the blue cross at the foot of Apparition Hill. It was good that we left early because it became very crowded very quickly; ten to twenty thousand people from all over the world travel to Medjugorje to be present for the monthly apparition when Our Blessed Mother appears and gives her message to Mirjana.

We had heard people speculating about why the cross was painted blue; people said it was because blue is Our Blessed Mother's favorite color. However, we would later learn from Mirjana's interpreter, Miki, that it was the only color available when the cross was being made—such a humble little cross to mark the location of Our Lady's visits.

In the throng of people, Julie and I became separated and our whole group was dispersed through the immense crowd. I found a spot amongst a group of Italian people on a rocky ledge. The rocks were precariously loose, and I could tell that this Italian family wasn't at all pleased that I had encroached on their space. But there really was room for me at that point, and they eventually relaxed. As more people pushed onto the hillside, the original inhabitants of our location became cranky and began bickering in Italian with the people all around them. I thought, "What will the Blessed Mother think when she arrives if these people are fighting amongst themselves?" What's more, the rocks were so unsteady that I was sure we were all going to fall over backward down the hillside. In fact, I was standing on a large stone that wobbled so badly that I needed to hold onto my closest neighbors for support or risk falling. Nevertheless, as we waited, we sang and prayed Rosaries. I was even able to begin the singing a couple of times, which seemed to win the admiration of my Italian neighbors so much so that they actually became friendly! Cramped and cold, we waited two hours for Mirjana to arrive, but it didn't matter. When she came, we could see her as she was escorted through the crowd to the foot of the blue cross. She prayed the Rosary with us and then Our Blessed Mother appeared to her and gave her a message. There was silence and a sense of peace that fell like a warm blanket over the hillside during the apparition. Afterward, Mirjana gave the message to her interpreter, Miki, who spoke it aloud in Croatian, English, and Italian:

> "Dear children! Also today I am among you to point you to the way that will help you to come to know God's love, the love of God who permitted

you to call Him Father and to perceive Him as Father.

"I ask of you to sincerely look into your hearts and to see how much you love Him. Is He the last to be loved? Surrounded by material goods, how many times have you betrayed, denied, and forgotten Him? My children, do not deceive yourselves with worldly goods. Think of your soul because it is more important than the body. Cleanse it.

"Invoke the Father. He is waiting for you. Come back to Him. I am with you because He, in His mercy, sends me. Thank you."

Mirjana, her guards, and her family worked their way through the crowd to leave, and some people from our tour group were close enough that they heard a woman thank Mirjana.

She stopped, looked at the woman, and said, "No, thank Our Blessed Mother and our Lord!"

Julie said that she saw deep love in Mirjana's eyes when she happened to look at her. There also now seemed to be a sense of loving kindness among the people on the hillside. Several people were pointing and when I looked to see what it was, I noticed that there was a cloud in the shape of a cross directly above Cross Mountain. The crowd began to disperse, and our group headed to St. James Church for the English Mass.

After Mass, we went to hear Patrick's talk at the castle, and while we were walking the grounds waiting for him, I happened to look into a small room through an open door. Inside, I saw an artist working on refinishing a full-size statue of the Pietá. It was completely white except for Jesus' hair and beard, which were brown. The artist said that the statue was more than 100 years old and she was removing the old paint to repaint it. She had already been working on it for two weeks. I looked at the face of Mary as she held the lifeless body of her precious Son. Then, I asked the artist if, as she worked on it, she would pray for Eric and our family. I explained to her what had happened and she said she would pray for us. A few minutes later, after I had walked away, she ran up to me and handed me a rosary made from Medjugorje stones.

"A family in Medjugorje makes these Rosaries," she said as she hugged me. "I would like you to have it."

I was humbled by this thoughtful gesture and thanked her.

As we continued to wait for Patrick, I asked Stephanie if I could share one of the songs I had written. The song, called "Like a Pearl," speaks about God's love for us in spite of our sinfulness; how He sees the pearl of beauty inside the ugliness of our sinful shells. I thought this song would be a good opener to Patrick's talk. Stephanie allowed me to sing it for our group and then Patrick shared his amazing conversion story with us.

Patrick is so full of the love of the Lord. During his talk, he bears his soul in such a humble, self-deprecating way, and anyone who recognizes sin in themselves would want the change that Patrick has experienced; he and his wife, Nancy, are accomplishing amazing work for the glory of God. When he finished his talk, I asked Patrick to pray for Eric and for our family. He hugged me and said he would.

It may seem strange that I would ask complete strangers to pray for Eric and our family; but, to me, it made perfect sense. I felt the need to gather as many prayer partners as possible because the weight of the burden of this cross was so crushing, and I knew that we needed all the help we could get. And so, every time someone agreed in such heartfelt compassion to pray for us, I felt peace. I knew we needed every prayer to get through this dark valley, and I was determined to cover us in as much prayer as possible.

When we left the castle, we went to hear Father Petar Ljubicic speak. He is the priest whom Mirjana has chosen to give the secrets to when it is time for them to be revealed. At that time, Father Petar will fast and pray, and then reveal a secret. Then, ten days after the revelation, the revealed event will occur.

Father Petar giving us his talk on November 2, 2009

During Father Petar's talk, he seemed to bounce on the balls of his feet. He is so filled with the Holy Spirit that he can hardly contain his passion and joy. Afterward, Julie and I were at the end of the exiting throng when Stephanie grabbed my arm and brought me to Father Petar. In Croatian, she explained to him what had happened to Eric and asked for his blessing. He nodded and began to reach toward my forehead. But even before he could reach my head, I fell backward, resting in the Spirit. At first, I was filled with pain. Deep sadness engulfed me, and I began to cry. Then, ever so slowly, I was filled with peace and I noticed the sensation of warmth throughout my womb. The place in which I had carried our babies was filled with warmth. I slowly rose, feeling refreshed and at peace. Later, I wondered if the sensation of warmth had been a blessing from the Lord on my motherhood. I sensed this was God's way of telling me that I had been a good mother.

I am so grateful for the many gifts and blessings that were poured out upon me and the other members of that pilgrimage tour, and I'm glad that Julie and I were able to share those incredible experiences together. Afterward, while journaling, I wrote the following prayer:

> I know that we will always hurt and sorrow over the loss of Eric, but we need not be in agony any longer. I do feel freer and it seems as though I am getting stronger. I want to be a better person because of Eric. I want to love as he did and be generous as he was.
>
> I want to say yes to the will of God in my life always. Lord, please help me to grow as I move forward in my faith journey. Blessed Mother, thank you so much for all you have done and are doing to draw your children ever closer to your Son, our Lord, Jesus.
>
> Thank you for the amazing gifts of peace, comfort, love, and HOPE! Please wrap your mantel around all the people I have ever known and draw us into your Immaculate Heart and into Jesus' Sacred Heart. Please continue to help Michael, Nathan, and Katherine in their healing process and in their conversions. I ask this in Jesus' name, by the power of the Holy Spirit and through the intercession of Our Blessed Mother, Mary.

When I returned home, I shared everything about the healing and blessings received in Medjugorje with Mike, Nathan, and Katherine. While the effects of these healing experiences stayed with us, the guilt about Eric's suicide and the devastation we felt because of our loss of him soon began to overshadow the peace we had received. Eventually, we would each need to find our own way to deal with our grief.

CHAPTER 11

Laura

It was November and Mike, Katherine, and I had agreed to participate in the National Catholic Youth Conference (NCYC) with a group of girls from our church. This conference takes place every two years in a different city in America, and we had planned to go before Eric died. Now, it was hard to follow through with those plans, but we couldn't back out.

For Mike, this was especially difficult. Originally, he was supposed to take Eric on a trip to Chicago during NCYC while I acted as a chaperone. Last time, I had accompanied Nathan and Katherine to Columbus, Ohio, along with some kids from our faith family at St. Joseph's back in Wisconsin. At that time, Mike and Eric had gone to Chicago together to explore the Museum of Science and Industry, visit friends, and have fun. Understandably, Mike just couldn't get that trip out of his mind. But this time would have to be different. Mike and I, another parent, and our parish youth minister would chaperone the trip to Kansas City, Kansas.

The night before we left for the NCYC trip, I had a dream of

Eric in heaven. In it, we were in our TV room downstairs. Eric was there, and he asked if I would scratch his back as he rested his head in my lap. In life, he had loved doing this and would always want the scratching to last longer than I was willing. I would begin feeling claustrophobic and would push him away after a while saying, "Okay, Eric, I need my space now." But, this time, I was determined that this moment together would last as long as he wanted, and I told myself to listen carefully to all he had to say. Eric always had so much he wanted to share that my ability to listen often ran out before he finished speaking. I asked him to tell me about heaven and promised myself that I wouldn't interrupt him as he spoke. He began by telling me what heaven looks like. As he spoke, I was suddenly with him in heaven, witnessing what he described! He showed me tall pillars of polished black stone lining the pathway to God's throne. I saw that the walkways in heaven were made of beautiful, huge, polished, flat rocks, which Eric loves to examine.

"Mommy," he said, "if I want, I can help find the rocks they use to make new pathways. Heaven's always under construction because they're always preparing for new arrivals."

He talked about the fact that he plays guitar in heaven, but he hadn't forgotten that he learned to play during his time on Earth, even commenting on his teacher Micah's great talent. In heaven, Eric has the best guitar he could ever have wanted. He loves playing guitar and growing in that skill. I saw him together with a group of kids—his new friends—playing their music for God.

"Sometimes, the angels join in and play with us," he told me. "But, mostly, they like to listen."

I could see angels joyfully watching and listening to Eric and his friends in their heavenly band. I had never seen Eric so happy!

As the dream continued, I learned that souls gain knowledge in heaven. We grow and learn during our earthly lives and we carry that knowledge with us to heaven. Then, when you visit with other souls there, you absorb their knowledge and they absorb yours; souls share freely with each other. Eric enjoys visiting with scientists and other people, absorbing the knowledge they share with him. He showed me a "laboratory" where souls can go to explore, experiment, and learn. He loves going there to gain knowledge. As we walked along together, other souls passed by us and I could feel the pure love, acceptance, and peace that Eric experiences in heaven.

"Mommy," he said, "I know that in my earthly life I was selfish sometimes. But, here in heaven, people are not selfish at all. They share everything and care for each other. They all love each other."

I could sense that, in heaven, there is pure goodness always.

I felt very peaceful when I awoke from this dream—as though I had actually visited with Eric—and I was amazed at all the ways his needs are met in heaven. His need for love, acceptance, and companionship—as well as his desire to share his creative, imaginative mind and his musical gifts—all are completely satisfied. Later, Mike told me that he had been praying for me—that, somehow, I would be relieved of the terrible

Mike, Laura, and Katherine at NCYC

burden of guilt I had been experiencing; that I would be reassured of Eric's new home in heaven; and that I could speak to him and let him know that I love him.

. . .

NCYC was wonderful, and we were glad we went. Looking back later, though, we realized that we were still in shock from Eric's death at that point. As time passed, the pain of the loss of Eric really began to sink in. The loneliness that parents feel for a child who dies is inexpressible. Our children are part of us, and when your child dies, it's like a big part of yourself is ripped away; the pain is excruciating. Each child is unique, precious, and irreplaceable. We miss Eric's presence with us. Our arms ache to hold him again, and our ears long to hear his voice. We miss his scent and his touch; nothing can fill the space he carved out for himself in our hearts. How could the depth of love that parents feel for their children be adequately expressed in words? It simply can't. Is it any wonder, then, that when a child dies, the parents find their loss unbearable?

During this time, I discovered that I needed to immerse myself in prayer to feel any peace, whereas Mike found it helpful to spend time praying at Eric's grave. He would go there by himself to pray, pour out his pain, and feel close to Eric. To this day, he still finds it helpful to go there, tend the flowers, and spend time in prayer.

A few days after Eric died, a friend gave us a silver coin with the words, "With God, all things are possible." We knew that it was only with God that we could hope to get through this horrible experience and go on to find happiness and become whole. Nonetheless, for a long time, we couldn't imagine ever being happy again; it was hard enough just to survive from one day to the next, and it took great effort to put one foot in front of the other and go through the motions of living. On our refrigerator, I taped a prayer card that we had received in a sympathy card at Eric's funeral. It reads, "Lord, please grant that we may hold dear the memory of your servant; never bitter for what we have lost, nor in regret of the past, but always in the hope of the eternal kingdom where you will bring us together again. We ask this in the name of Jesus Christ, our Lord. Amen." I took great comfort from this simple prayer and prayed it every day. It can still be found on our refrigerator.

Meanwhile, Mike, being the engineer that he is, formulated his "dot and line theory" of earthly versus eternal life after his first pilgrimage to Medjugorje. This theory taught him to keep focused on the never-ending line—a line representing our eternal life. In this life, we are tempted to focus on the dot, which represents our earthly life, but we knew that we had to stay focused on the line, which represents eternal life. We had to follow the words I had heard the morning after Eric died: "See him in life!" If we could focus on Eric in eternal life with the Lord, filled with His love, peace, and joy, then it just might help make this cross bearable.

I needed to keep moving. Being still for any length of time was difficult, as my mind would take me to places I didn't want it to go. However, after going for a walk, I felt so much better; I would bring a rosary in my pocket and pray it while walking. I read many books on suicide loss and finding hope and healing after the death of a loved one, as well as inspirational and spiritual books. I wanted to learn how other people who had suffered tragic experiences had survived. Along with many others, the book *Grieving a Suicide: A Loved One's Search for Comfort, Answers and Hope* by Albert Y. Hsu was so helpful for me in the search for peace and hope.

Mike and I tried to be sensitive to each other's grieving styles; it can be really difficult for parents to understand that they each have their own way of dealing with the loss of their child. So, we learned to be patient with each other and allow each other to grieve in our own ways.

We attended grief support groups and workshops as often as we could. There, we saw that people with faith seemed better able to handle tragic loss, as opposed to those without faith, who seemed more likely to be stuck in their grieving and unable to move forward into acceptance and healing. Additionally, one of our greatest comforts came from the prayers and loving actions of family, friends, and even acquaintances. The caring concern we received was a great comfort.

I also found comfort and peace through journaling. As I look back now on the entries in my journal, I can see that, over time, the excruciating pain was lifting. A scab had begun to form over my wound. And, although there will always be a deep scar on our hearts from Eric's death, we were learning to live with it. The following are entries from my journal:

April 2, 2010, Good Friday – late at night

Dear Eric,

How are you? I wish I could see you as you are now. I wonder what it is like for you, living in heaven. Dad, Nathan, and I drove over to Wisconsin today for Easter weekend. Katherine left last Wednesday with the high school choir to go to Orlando, Fl. They will sing there a couple of times and have fun at Disney World.

Do you remember when Dad and I surprised you kids with our trip to Florida? You were only 3 years old. I wonder, if we could talk together, what you would remember about that trip.

Anyway, I especially didn't want to be at home for this Easter with you and Katherine both gone. Uncle Don and Aunt Julie invited us to come over for Easter when they came to help us surprise Dad on his birthday. We decided to take them up on it.

It feels good to be with them, although it is weird to be just Dad and me here. We dropped Nathan off at the Stevens' house in our old neighborhood. We ate at China Buffet tonight. Remember how good the food is there? You always loved that restaurant, especially the cantaloupe melon. After dinner, we went for a walk to Narrows Park, "Matchstick Park," as you kids called it when you were young. Being there brought back memories of us playing there through the years. It was a favorite when we would have "kids choice day." You liked the swinging horses and the seesaws very much. You and Katherine always played on those together.

You enjoyed walking along the cement ledge at the edge of the lake; it made me nervous when you were little. I remembered pushing you on the swings here. I became sad as these memories came flooding back, Eric. We have so many memories stored in the surroundings here. Scenes of your growing-up years continue to flash through my mind. We had a good life here. All we can do now is pray that Jesus will continue to help us face each new day as we try to learn how to live without you.

I hate being without you! So much joy is gone. Time is passing. In 11 days from now, it will be seven months ago that you died. For the first time since you died, we will go to St. Joseph's Church on Easter Sunday. Nathan said, "Of all the people who will be there, we have the greatest reason to be rejoicing because of what Jesus did for us, dying on the cross and rising to new life—defeating death and making eternal life possible for us all."

I know this is true. It is just still too fresh for me to be happy about you being gone from us for the rest of our earthly lives. I looked forward to the future with you, Eric. Now, you will not be physically a part of that future and your absence hurts.

*I wish I would have appreciated you more when you were here. I wish I could look back on the times we shared with **NO** regrets. I love you, Eric. Please know this fact deep within you. Please help me to follow the advice in these prayers:*

"Lord Jesus, help me to hold dear the memory of your servant, never bitter for what I have lost nor in regret of the past, but always in the hope of the eternal kingdom where you will bring us together again."

"God, grant me the serenity to accept the things I cannot change, the courage to change the things I can, and the wisdom to know the difference."

What a beautiful gift Don and Julie have given us to allow us to come here for our first Easter without you! They must have known this would be a difficult time for us, yet they were not afraid to be exposed to our sadness. They willingly changed any plans they may have had to accommodate our needs. We are truly blessed by their friendship and love. Thank you, Lord.

Good night, Eric. I love you.

P.S. Springtime is upon us. We've had temperatures in

*the mid-70s. All snow is gone. Last Sunday, Dad,
Nathan, and I went on a 4-wheeler ride to check out the
flooding of the Big Sioux River from the snow melt.
Katherine was gone on a SEARCH weekend.*

*Do you know these things, Eric? I wonder how close
you are to us. Can you see us going on with our lives? Do
you pray for our needs? I think you do. I pray that you
enjoy every moment of this, your first Easter celebration in
heaven.*

April 4, 2010 – Easter

Dear Eric,

*Today is Easter Sunday. Nathan, Dad, and I went to
Mass at St. Joseph's Church, the church in which you were
baptized and grew up. We sat in our old spot beside the
choir. We greeted Father Jim and a few old friends. It was
8:30 Mass, not the Mass we usually attended, but we had
plans to meet Uncle Don's family at a restaurant for
dinner.*

*It was both comforting and painful for me to be there.
In a way, it was fitting for us to be in our old spot, like you
were there with us. It was painful, though, to be there
without you for the first time. The words of Mass were
comforting: Jesus is risen! He has defeated death and
opened the gates of heaven to us. You have entered into
everlasting life! I am happy for you, but it hurts so much to
live without you.*

*When Mass was over, as we walked out of church, I
was noticing the bright blue sky. It had been overcast and*

rainy earlier in the morning. I saw an eagle flying in the sky over the church playground where you played so many times in your childhood.

It reminded me and Dad of how our friend Lenny Locke saw two eagles swoop down over his head the week after you died. The sight had caused him to think of the song, "On Eagle's Wings." He didn't know it, but we had that song sung by the high school choir at your funeral.

Dad said that surely must be a sign. It was very comforting to watch that eagle. It reminded me of when we first stepped into our house on Rudolph Road. It was being built and we were looking to buy. You were not quite two years old. We had to hold you so that you wouldn't get hurt on the construction site. We walked up the stairs in the split-level house and went to look out the windows that overlooked the lake in the back yard. There, we saw two eagles soaring in the sky over the lake. I knew this was to be our home. You grew up there until we moved to South Dakota.

You now have a new home, Eric.

Please pray that, one day, Daddy, Nathan, Katherine, and I will be able to join you there.

I love you, Eric.

Happy Easter, my precious boy! Love you always!
Mommy

CHAPTER 12

"When the just cry out, the Lord hears them, and from all their distress He rescues them. The Lord is close to the brokenhearted; and those who are crushed in spirit He saves."
(Psalm 34:18-19)

Laura

The year 2010 was a healing year for us. For starters, it was a big traveling year for our family. In addition to Katherine going to Florida with the high school choir before Easter, later that month, Mike, Katherine, and I went on a trip to Taiwan. Mike worked with a Taiwanese company that is owned by a woman and run by her son. The son was getting married and wanted Mike to come and be the guest of honor at his wedding reception. However, Mike didn't feel right leaving us, and when he mentioned it, they invited all of us to come. Unfortunately, Nathan was unable to get away because of school, so the three of us went.

It was amazing to experience Taiwanese culture. We went to the top of Taipei 101, one of the tallest buildings in the world; we were treated to sumptuous meals; we had a wonderful time on a boat ride to a national park where people performed music; and we visited a temple while walking beautiful pathways where poinsettia plants grew wild. We enjoyed new food there, too, like eggs that had been hardboiled in tea. We also rode a bullet train from Taipei to Chiayi City, where the wedding reception was held. The train ride turned a three-hour car ride into a one-hour flight on rails. We were also able to enjoy more culture when we walked through the night market in Chiayi City. Here, there were vendor stalls with an unimaginable variety of foods, clothing, and other goods for sale. It was like being at a Taiwanese carnival!

We were treated like royalty by our kind hosts. Being present for the festivities at the wedding reception was a once-in-a-lifetime experience; each entrée they served looked so much like a work of art that I was actually sad to destroy it by eating it. Our hosts laughed when I took pictures of the exquisite dishes. We were truly blessed to have been given this experience; it was a refreshing reprieve from the constant weight of the cross that we were bearing. After our return from this trip, the Lord would provide further assistance in lifting the weight of our cross.

Katherine, Mike, and Laura at a wedding celebration in Taiwan

Over the years, our involvement in the Catholic Charismatic Renewal would prove to be a great comfort. We enjoy the gift of being able to grow in our relationship with God through this movement of the Holy Spirit. The usual format of a meeting consists of singing praise and worship music; praying through intercessory prayer for the needs of our members, families, friends, and community; hearing prepared teachings; being led by the Holy Spirit to pray in tongues and prophesy; breaking into small groups for faith-sharing; and praying over one another. We also find random readings from the Bible and are often amazed to see how the Lord uses readings from all over the Bible and ties them together into one theme that He impresses upon us. We feel the presence of God during these meetings and, in profound ways, God reaches out to us to build up the body of His Church and sustain us in His love. Through the Renewal, we have learned how to be open to the Holy Spirit working in and through us. In fact, we probably would not have recognized many of the manifestations of God's love and faithfulness that have come to us over the years had we not been prepared ahead of time through our experiences in the Catholic Charismatic Renewal.

In my May 22, 2010, journal entry, I shared examples of how the Holy Spirit worked through the Renewal to help us heal:

We had our monthly Life in The Spirit meeting at St. Thomas More last Thursday night.

I wanted to skip it because I was feeling down, but Mike insisted we go. I am glad he did.

During the meeting, we talked about how Satan is always ready to bring us down, especially through negative self-talk and in the trials we face. We really need to hold on tight to our faith and to the Lord for strength to wage our battle with the foe.

Messages received while being prayed over were:
"I am always with you."
"I am leading you."
"I am carrying you at this time."
"I am not done with you."
"You must complete the tasks I have set for you."
"Be not afraid."
"You are my precious daughter."
"Give me your broken heart."

While people were sharing these messages, I saw myself giving Jesus the broken pieces of my heart. He tenderly received them, healed my broken heart, and gave it back to me.

Mike and I went down to the monthly Bread of Life prayer group meeting in Sioux Falls. During the prayer time, prayer group members received messages that Jesus wanted to give us. He wanted to fill us with His love, mercy, peace, and more. In my mind, I saw a large, gray, clay pot shattered on the floor. There were shards and pieces everywhere, and I knew that this was me in my brokenness.

I thought, "How can you fill me when I am shattered?"

Jesus responded, "Give me the pieces."

A few days later, as I was praying in the chapel, I asked the Lord, "What do you want me to do?"

His answer was, "Heal."

Mike and I felt it would be a good thing for the healing of our family if we could all go on a pilgrimage together. We looked into going to Medjugorje with Stephanie Percic, but were disappointed to learn that Nathan and Katherine couldn't get away from school for the dates Stephanie had available. So, we found a tour agency advertised in the *Medjugorje Magazine* and decided to sign up for a trip that would include Italy and Medjugorje. In Italy, we would see Rome's Major Basilicas and be present for an audience with the Pope. We would also visit Lanciano, Loreto, Assisi, Monte Cassino, Saint Michael's Cave, and San Giovanni Rotondo, in addition to spending five nights in Medjugorje. We felt that this would be a great opportunity for healing, but we could never have imagined all that the Lord would do to help strengthen us for our journey into the future.

Our pilgrimage began in Rome. On Tuesday, May 25, 2010, the second day of the pilgrimage, we visited St. Peter's Basilica in Rome. The history of this beautiful place and the awesome artwork is truly breathtaking. We were able to walk past the tombs of Pope John Paul II, as well as many other saints. We also saw Michelangelo's masterpiece—the Pietá—and the Sistine Chapel, along with countless other beautiful works of art in the Vatican museum.

Our family at St. Peter's Basilica in Rome

Our tour guide mentioned that we would be celebrating Mass in St. Peter's Basilica that day, and I hoped that we might be able to get seats inside the magnificent structure, but God had bigger plans; that evening, we attended a Mass celebrating the 50th anniversary of the priesthood of a cardinal! He actually presided over the Mass and we received communion in front of the altar under which St. Peter is buried. We were exhilarated that our family was able to participate in this blessed event. The next day, we attended the Wednesday weekly Papal audience and were present with thousands of other people to hear Pope Benedict XVI speak. Something he said really impressed me:

"Jesus showed His power by washing His disciples' feet. He showed His kingship through the cross. We need to follow Jesus' example of servant leader."

Then, along with all the people there, we received the Pope's blessing.

Nathan—who was a history major in college and has loved history since he was a very little boy—was perturbed that, here we were in Rome, yet we were not exploring sites of purely historic significance; he desperately wanted to see the Coliseum. And, although the tour guides hadn't planned on going to that part of the city, at Nathan's insistence, they decided to let us out for lunch across the street from the Coliseum. We walked around it and took pictures while enjoying panini sandwiches and gelato. It was exciting to see the ruins of

Nathan and Katherine outside the Coliseum

the ancient city, and we were thankful that our guides had changed the tour route so that we could do this. We agreed that we should return here someday as tourists and learn about all the historically significant sights.

After lunch, we visited other major basilicas in Rome and had some beautiful spiritual moments in these churches, including St. Mary Major, St. John Lateran, The Basilica of the Holy Cross in Jerusalem, and the Scala Sancta—The Holy Staircase. The Holy Stairs are believed to be the stairs that Jesus climbed to be judged by Pilot. They were brought to Rome from Jerusalem, and pilgrims are encouraged to climb the stairs prayerfully on their knees.

Mike

Mike at the top of the Holy Stairs

I had been helping Rosemary, a woman on our tour who was wheelchair bound. It seemed as though I wouldn't get a chance to climb the stairs because I had been left to watch over her possessions while she went up. However, I knew we needed to get to the bus, so I prayed and asked God that, if it were not against His will, to allow me to go up the stairs, but if this was not to be, I would accept that. After the prayer, someone came and took my place, so I began to climb the stairs. Small, Plexiglas windows are embedded in the stairs, and one can look through them to see where drops of Christ's blood fell. As I climbed the stairs on my knees, I prayed, crying more every step as I thought of Eric. Then, when I was on the last couple of steps, I looked into the little window on the very last one. There, looking back at me, I saw the face of Jesus wearing the crown of thorns. I thought it was a holographic picture, and I noticed that Jesus' eyes in this image followed me as I continued up the stairs; His head even turned to face me directly.

When we returned to the bottom of the stairs, as I pushed Rosemary's wheelchair back toward the bus, I pondered aloud, "I wonder why they had that picture of Jesus in the glass window on the top step?"

Everyone looked at each other then said to me, "What picture of Jesus?"

That's when we realized that I had seen something no one else had. I knew then that I had witnessed something extremely special.

Laura

Saint Helena, the mother of Emperor Constantine the Great, went to the Holy Land and brought numerous relics back to Rome. Many of these relics are located in the Church of Jerusalem, where we saw: the cross beam of the cross of Saint Dismas, the "good thief" who was crucified with Jesus; nails used in Christ's crucifixion; thorns from His crown of thorns; and a relic of the finger of Saint Thomas, which he had placed in Jesus' wounds. There is also a replica of the Shroud of Turin and a crucifix based on the wounds depicted on the Shroud. As I prayed before the crucifix that portrays Our Lord with the wounds made evident on the Shroud of Turin, I heard the words,

"Be filled with my joy. I have paid the price for your sin." I felt a deep sense of peace fill my soul.

On Thursday, May 27, we visited Monte Cassino, an abbey founded by St. Benedict in the fifth century. Beneath the main altar are the tombs of Saint Benedict and his sister, Saint Scholastica. Nathan was very interested in this stop for its significance to World War II; this was the scene of the Battle of Monte Cassino or the Battle for Rome in 1944, a battle the Allies fought against the Axis forces during the Italian Campaign of World War II. The hill is 1,706.04 feet tall and it's possible to see a great distance from the top. The monastery there was destroyed in bombing raids by the Allies, but rebuilt after the war. We then drove from Monte Cassino through the Italian countryside and arrived in the little town of Mugnano Del Cardinale Avellino, where we saw the Sanctuary of Saint Philomena. There lie relics of 13-year-old Saint Philomena, who was martyred for defending her purity for Jesus. Standing before her relics, I was thinking about Eric and asking Saint Philomena to pray for him. "He is with the Lord," I heard her say in my mind, and I could feel the strength and power of the Holy Spirit all around me in this place. We gave a picture of Eric to the caretaker priest there and he graciously said that he would place it with Saint Philomena's remains.

From there, we traveled through the hills to the plain at the Adriatic Seacoast. Then, our bus trekked up a mountainside as we looked out over the beautiful coast and endless groves of olive trees. We had arrived at Saint Michael's Cave. Saint Michael the Archangel is said to have appeared here several times to various people over hundreds of years. We celebrated Mass inside the cave; some say that a person can pray for anything in Saint Michael's Cave and it will be given, as long as it doesn't go against the will of God.

Mike

I had been praying during this pilgrimage because I needed something, some confirmation from the Lord to reassure me that Eric was okay and that he was in heaven. It was during our time at Saint Michael's Cave that this prayer became refined. I began praying for a specific blessing, saying, "God, I need something! I need something really big. When we are in Medjugorje, I want to see a visionary, and I want to be invited to his or her apparition, and during the apparition I want to see the Blessed Mother with Eric standing next to her. I need something that big, God, or something like that so my mind can be at peace. I hate to ask this, God, but I need something really big like that." I said this, pouring out all my heart and with many tears.

We finished the day with a drive to San Giovanni Rotunda, the place Padre Pio called home. He lived there for many years and also died there. Being in Saint Pio's hometown reminded me of Eric because he thought Padre Pio may have been his patron saint. I had learned in Medjugorje that if you pray before going to sleep at night to know the name of your patron saint—your personal saint who watches out for you in a special way—then, in the morning, you will know your saint's name. Eric thought his was either Padre Pio or Rosa Parks, he wasn't sure which. We still wonder what it was like for Eric to actually get to meet both of his guardians in heaven.

Laura

Our group prayed the Rosary on the way from our hotel to San Giovanni Rotunda. We looked around the grounds of the holy place, including the tomb of Saint Padre Pio, which is in a beautiful chapel. Katherine and I filed past the Saint's tomb in a long line of people. You can even reach your hand through an iron-grated window and touch his tomb while praying for his intercession. We did, and then Katherine went off by herself to pray in the chapel. However, I was deeply feeling the pain and guilt I usually felt when I thought about Eric's death, so I looked to see if one of our priests might be available for confession. Just then, I saw Father Royanna, one of our spiritual directors on the trip, approaching me. He had just finished his turn touching Padre Pio's tomb. He told me that when he touched the tomb, he had had a vision.

"Laura, I saw Eric with God," he told me. "God called Eric. He needed him. Eric was innocent. God knows that."

Father Royanna could not have known how much I needed to hear those words at that moment, and it was so soothing to my aching heart to hear him share his vision of Eric with the Lord.

Later, we attended Mass in a chapel just a few feet from where St. Pio's body had been laid temporarily before the completion of his beautiful final resting place. A priest who had been an assistant to Padre Pio during the last few years of his life spoke and then offered that Father Albano, another of our spiritual directors, could bless each of us with Padre Pio's crucifix and one of his gloves, which he had worn over the nail marks of the stigmata he received as a young priest. We were amazed to have the opportunity to receive this great blessing.

On May 29, after this visit to San Giovanni Rotundo, we took an overnight ferry across the Adriatic Sea to Split, Croatia, and drove three

Fr. Albano blesses Nathan with one of Padre Pio's gloves

hours through breathtakingly beautiful, mountainous terrain to Medjugorje. Mike and I were so happy to be in Medjugorje with Nathan and Katherine. During the bus ride there, we learned that, for two of our five nights there, we would be staying at the home of the visionary Mirjana! When Mike heard this news, he was encouraged that his prayer to see Eric with the Blessed Mother Mary might just be granted. We recognized the amazing grace of being invited to stay in the home of Mirjana so that our children could meet a person who experiences apparitions and speaks with Our Blessed Mother. When we arrived, Mirjana welcomed us into her home and helped serve our lunch. She was very humble and kind.

Lord God,
source and destiny of our lives,
in your loving providence
you gave us Eric Walter
to grow in wisdom, age, and grace.
Now you have called him to yourself.

As we grieve over the loss of one so young,
we seek to understand your purpose.

Draw him to yourself
and give him full stature in Christ.
May he stand with all the angels and saints,
who know your love and praise your saving will.

We ask this through Christ our Lord, in whom we
trust and dedicate our lives
Amen

Eric's funeral flyer and the picture that brought a fellow pilgrim a vision of Eric in heaven

After lunch on our second day in Medjugorje, I took Mirjana aside and told her our story. I asked if she would please pray for Eric's soul and for our family's healing. She hugged me and said she would. Later that day, as Mike walked through the fields after a visit to the Risen Cross, a fellow pilgrim from our group came up to him and said he had something he wanted to share.

"A few days ago when we were in Italy, Laura told me what happened to Eric and showed me the flyer from Eric's funeral," he said. "When I saw the picture of Eric as a little boy on the back cover, I had an experience that I've never had before. I had a vision where I saw Eric; that he is with the Lord in heaven, and that God allowed him to come home. Eric was innocent! The Lord has a job for Eric. He will be at heaven's gates to greet you when you arrive there one day."

Mike shared this beautiful confirmation with me, and I marveled at the ways the Lord uses each of us to help one another on our life's journey! This was now the third person to share the message that Eric is in heaven, that he is innocent, and that the Lord called him home and has a job for him to do. The first time we received this message was right after Eric's death when a woman from one of Mike's earlier pilgrimages sent him a letter mentioning that while she was in deep prayer during adoration, she saw a vision of Eric in heaven. She said that Eric was innocent, and that God had allowed him to come, and that he has a special purpose. The second time was when Father Royanna told me the same thing at San Giovanni Rotunda, and now we had heard it a third time in Medjugorje. It would have been wonderful to hear this once, but to have it confirmed three times by three different people was amazing!

The next morning, May 31st, Mirjana spoke to our group in the dining room of her home. She told us her experience with the apparitions and shared the influence that the messages had had on her life and what the Blessed Mother says to mankind through her messages. Here are some notes I took while listening to her that morning:

> The one who feels Mary as Mother and God as Father has no fear of anything. We should be ready at this very moment for the coming of God.

Our Lady asks for our help to change unbelievers through our prayers and example. Pray for unbelievers. Do not preach. We must talk with our life so unbelievers can see God in our life. This is the time of decisions. God's children have great responsibility. We mustn't judge others, but pray for them and set an example.

The most important message from Mary: "Attend Holy Mass. My Son is with you." She also says, "Pray so that I can pray to my Son for you." Jesus comes first. Our Lady sees us all as her children, each with our own special mission. Have your heart open.

Our Lady always says something about the importance of priests. The most important blessing is from priests. Pray for priests. Do not judge your priest. Take your rosary and pray for them. People judge so much. There is so little love. Our Lady wishes us to be judged by our love.

Nothing can unite families as when we pray together. Parents put seeds of faith into their children. Show them the importance of Mass and prayer by setting an example.

Our Lady desires to give us her Son. If we don't have peace, we have nothing. The only true peace is Jesus and this is what Our Lady desires to give us—true peace.

Answers to our questions come from prayer. Surrender to Jesus with complete confidence and He will reveal what He desires from you. Everyone who claims to love God should have mercy in his or her heart.

All people have their own crosses to bear. Our prayer helps us to carry our cross. Be with others to help them with their crosses. Do not be afraid to follow Jesus. Nothing that causes good will be denied from you. Do not look for peace in wrong things. Look for peace in Jesus. Eternal life and eternal peace can only be found in Jesus.

Love others. Pray for them. Place them in our Mother's hands. Set an example with your life. Show others you are different by the way you live your own life. Never judge others. Let them see your love, joy, and peace. You are called to spread the love of God further.

Truly Catholic people have Mass. They live their faith. We have to have an open heart and seek relationship with Jesus and Blessed Mother.

It is most important to thank our dear God who sends Our Blessed Mother to be with us all these years. This is God's great love!

These are the actions Our Blessed Mother asks of us to help us grow in holiness:

·   *Fast on bread and water on Wednesdays and Fridays. Offer this for the conversion of sinners and the salvation of souls.*

·   *Attend Holy Mass.*

·   *Pray from the heart, especially the Rosary.*

·   *Read the Bible.*

·   *Go to monthly confession because, "Only a pure heart can be open to receive the gifts the Lord wishes to give it."*

Pope John Paul II told Mirjana, "Medjugorje is hope for the entire world. Now Medjugorje is in the hands of the Vatican. What comes from God, no one can stop."

Mike

During her talk, Mirjana asked if anyone had any questions. At one point, I started by saying to Mirjana that she has met my wife, Laura, and our two children, Nathan and Katherine, but we also had a younger child whom we recently lost.

I struggled then and began to say, "I would like to know if the Blessed Mother has ever said anything about people who have died..." and then I paused.

"You do not need to finish as I know what you want to ask," Mirjana said. "I will speak with you privately after our talk with the group."

Afterwards, it was time for our group to move out of Mirjana's home to the place where we would stay for the remaining three nights. However, before we left, we were to meet outside for a group picture. As I came outside, Mirjana took me aside, called her interpreter, Miki, and told me that she wanted Laura and me to be standing beside her at the blue cross for the apparition she would experience on June 2nd. She instructed Miki to come get us and help us maneuver through the huge crowd of 10,000 to 20,000 people so we could be next to her when Our Blessed Mother came to visit and give her monthly message to Mirjana. We were speechless! I realized that this could be the fulfillment of the prayer request I had made back in Saint Michael's Cave; it was such a huge blessing! Unfortunately, we were disappointed to learn that, because of the large crowds, Nathan and Katherine would not be able to join us with Mirjana. But we knew that the graces we received from this blessing would be poured out on them, as well.

That morning, June 2, was bright and sunny, with a slight chill in the air. I was certain that God was answering my prayer to see

Eric with the Blessed Mother Mary. In fact, I was so certain that I asked Nathan and Katherine if they wanted me to deliver a message to Eric for them.

Thousands of people come from around the world to be present on the second day of each month when Mirjana receives her apparition and message from the Blessed Mother Mary. Many people actually stake a claim by staying on the hillside the night before the apparition so they can be as close as possible to Mirjana during Our Blessed Mother's visit.

Fortunately, as promised, Miki came and escorted Laura and me—as well as the woman I had been helping throughout the pilgrimage—through the impenetrable crowd. Rope barriers on either side of the path made it very narrow and getting through the crowd to the blue cross was extremely difficult. However, Miki is in charge of directing traffic, especially near where Mirjana kneels to receive the apparition. So, when we arrived at the blue cross, he placed us in front of some Italian women who had already selected their choice location. It was clear that they weren't at all happy to be dislodged from their positions; one of them even began to let us know this by poking me in the back with her umbrella until one of Mirjana's assistants spoke with her. Later, the crowd all joined in praying the Rosary as we waited for Mirjana to arrive, and I looked around at the crowd surrounding us: I saw a father holding his son, who looked both disabled and gravely ill; I also noticed a mother holding a baby girl who was about a year old and who appeared to be near death. At the same time, Mirjana's guards were turning away people in wheelchairs, on crutches, and with various illnesses because there wasn't room for anyone else to enter the crowded space. In that moment, I had a sudden and confident realization that I didn't need to see Eric with Our Blessed Mother because I knew that he was in heaven. Instead, I wanted to give up my spot to one of the people who was being turned away. This was a huge sacrifice for me because I really believed that I was about to see Eric with the Blessed Mother! So, I called Miki over and explained that I wanted to give up my spot. When he asked why and I told him, he gently patted me on the chest.

"Mike, you don't understand," he said. "Mirjana said that you need to be here now. Let God take care of you as He plans and trust that God will take care of the others in His time."

With that, I stayed in my place and joined in praying the Rosary. Later, when we were coming back down the hill after the apparition, I realized that I had received my healing before the Blessed Mother even made her appearance; I had been healed at the moment I was willing to sacrifice my place to someone else by truly believing that I was going to see Eric. I also saw God's wisdom in the fact that I didn't get exactly what I had prayed for; I understood that if God had answered my prayer in the way I had asked, I would have felt very guilty—who was I to ask for something so profound? What right did I have to make such a request when other people were suffering so greatly? God allowed me to be healed and to believe without seeing, just as Jesus said:

"Blessed are those who believe without seeing!" (John 20:29)

Laura

When Mirjana arrived, I stood behind her husband and Mike stood behind me. We were just a few feet away from her when she and her close loved ones all knelt down and joined in praying the Rosary. After praying, Mirjana suddenly looked up with a huge smile on her face and the crowd became silent. A feeling of peace and love enveloped us and everyone was quiet as Mirjana conversed with the Mother of Jesus. I sensed a blanket of peace wrapping around us, stretching out from the hillside in all directions and out over Medjugorje and beyond. At times, Mirjana looked joyful, but at other times, she seemed sad. She listened intently, occasionally nodding her head and there were tears rolling down her face. When it was over, Mirjana covered her face with her hands as the praying of the Rosary resumed. Then, when she was ready, Mirjana shared with Miki what Mary, Our Lady Queen of Peace, had said to her, which Miki shared in Croatian, Italian, and English. When Miki spoke Our Lady's message in English, I couldn't believe my ears! I felt as though Mary had orchestrated our pilgrimage in order that we would be present to hear her words, and as if she was speaking directly to us through Mirjana. This is the message she gave:

> "Dear children, today I call you, with fasting and prayer, to clear the way by which my Son will enter into your hearts. Accept me as a mother and a messenger of God's love and of His desire for your salvation. Free yourself of everything from the past which burdens you and gives you a sense of guilt; of everything that brought you to error— darkness. Accept the light. Be born anew in the justice of my Son. Thank you."

As Miki spoke the words that the Blessed Mother had said to Mirjana, I could almost see Mary smiling and gently wagging her finger at me like a mother scolding her small child, saying, "Now, that is enough feeling guilty. You need to stop that." The weight of the guilt lifted off my shoulders; if the Blessed Mother said I must free myself of the burden of guilt I had been carrying, I had better listen to her! I felt a lightness of spirit that I hadn't felt for a very long time.

It's still difficult to believe that we have been blessed so abundantly. Being able to stay at Mirjana's home and hear her speak to us personally about Medjugorje; being asked to join her for the apparition; Mike's healing prior to Our Lady's appearance;

and the message itself, which was exactly what I needed to hear. It was really beyond our wildest imaginings, and it made me think of Psalm 116:12:

"How can I make a return to the Lord for the good He has done for me?"

Our pilgrimage concluded with visits to Cupertino, Loreto, Torentino, and Assisi, Italy, where we were introduced to saints we had never heard of and walked in the footsteps of Saint Francis and Saint Claire. We also walked through the basilica dedicated to Saint Francis and visited San Damiano—the church Saint Francis rebuilt—where Saint Claire lived and died. So many blessings and graces were poured out on us during this trip that it would end up taking us a long time to absorb and appreciate it all.

Nathan and Katherine on Cross Mountain

CHAPTER 13

Laura

Time went on and, as the months passed, we approached the first anniversary of Eric's death. On July 24, the Nelson side of our family gathered together at my brother Dan's home so we could commemorate what would have been Eric's 15th birthday; we were glad to have the company of family during the first of Eric's birthdays without him.

A few weeks later—Sunday, August 8, 2010—was our 24th wedding anniversary, and one of Eric's classmates had arranged for two Masses to be said for Eric: one on his birthday and the second on our anniversary. It was a beautiful gift, and the last song at Mass on the morning of our anniversary happened to be "Joyful, Joyful, We Adore Thee,"[1] the gathering hymn from our wedding, which no one would have known. The words of the first verse were very comforting:

> *"Joyful, joyful, we adore Thee, God of glory, Lord of love.*
> *Hearts unfold like flowers before Thee, opening to the sun above.*
> *Melt the clouds of sin and sadness. Drive the dark of doubt away.*
> *Giver of immortal gladness, fill us with the light of day."*

Later that evening, we heard wonderful news from our friend Bob Rogalla from Wisconsin. Bob and his wife, Anna, have children the same ages as ours, and their youngest son, Nick, was Eric's age. Bob shared that Nick was at Eucharistic Adoration during a retreat, and as the priest processed toward him with the monstrance containing the consecrated host, Nick saw a bright light coming from the monstrance. He felt numb and couldn't feel his body, and then he saw Eric dressed in a white robe! He said he was surrounded by clouds and was standing in front of golden gates. Nick said Eric smiled and was happy, but that he didn't speak. Nick was shaken by this experience because he had never had one before, but he and his parents felt it was important for him to share this with us, and we were so glad they did! What an awesome gift to receive on our anniversary! Eric always loved giving gifts, and it seemed as though he was continuing his gift-giving from heaven.

As the first anniversary of Eric's death loomed closer, our sadness increased. We were constantly thinking, "This time last year, we were…" Our longing for him was unbearable, and Sunday, September 12, was the most difficult. We went to church just as we had the year before and, incredibly, the Mass readings were about the lost sheep and the prodigal son, and we sang "On Eagle's Wings" and "The Prayer of St. Francis." Father Rod's homily also proclaimed God's great mercy and, for us, this all pointed to Eric. However, as evening approached, I was feeling especially sad and I thought about how, at this time the year before, Mike and I were trap shooting. So, we went down to the chapel at our church and prayed the Glorious Mysteries of the Rosary. I looked for the Lord to speak to us through His Holy Word and let the Bible fall open. My eyes rested on 2 Corinthians 4:8-18, where St. Paul writes:

"We are afflicted in every way but not constrained, perplexed but not driven to despair, persecuted but not abandoned, struck down, but not

destroyed; always carrying about in the body the dying of Jesus, so that the life of Jesus may also be manifested in our body… Therefore, we are not discouraged; rather, although our outer self is wasting away, our inner self is being renewed day by day. For this momentary light affliction is producing for us an eternal weight of glory beyond all comparison as we look not to what is seen but to what is unseen; for what is seen is transitory, but what is unseen is eternal."

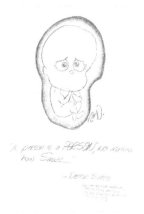

I was thinking about the power and meaning of this reading when I noticed a bookmark tucked into the pages of the Bible. As I picked it up and looked at it, I was amazed when I saw another gift that Eric had left us. Eric was *very* pro-life and, as his classmate had pointed out in her letter to us, he had demonstrated this in cards with funny phrases. Her favorite was one in which Eric had quoted Dr. Seuss, "A person's a person no matter how small." This young woman is a very good artist, and she had drawn a cartoon figure of a cute little baby in the uterus of its mother with the caption Eric had shared with her from Dr. Seuss. Randi Neilsen[2] sent this to us after Eric died.

The bookmark I found in the Bible that day showed a photograph of a six-week-old embryo with the caption reading, "A person is a person no matter how small." It was a beautiful reminder of Eric's beliefs and the friends whose lives he had touched.

The next day, September 13, 2010, was the first anniversary of Eric's death. Mike and I took a vase of Eric's favorite white roses from the front of our house to the cemetery, placed them beside his headstone and prayed the Divine Mercy Chaplet for him. Then, we drove down to Trinity Heights retreat center in Sioux

City, Iowa, where we prayed for Eric, requested masses to be offered for him, and prayed for our family's continued healing. We had invited Nathan and Katherine to join us in these activities, but they each decided to commemorate the anniversary in their own way.

As time goes on, we all continue to find our own ways to remember Eric. Although waves of pain still engulf us on occasion, we're learning to accept our lives without his presence. We enjoy telling stories about him and the times we shared with him; the countless prayers that others have offered and continue to offer for us have also been greatly helpful to us in our healing process.

Time is a strange thing. Often, when we think about moments that we shared with Eric, it seems like they occurred just moments ago. Yet, when we look at all that has transpired since he left us, it feels like he has been gone for a very, very long time. Holidays, birthdays, and the anniversary of his death magnify the burden of the loss and intensify the pain. As Christmas passed and we found ourselves in 2011, I was feeling especially low. One day, as I sat in Eric's bedroom, missing him and crying, I turned to the Bible once again, hoping the Lord would give words of comfort—and He did just that with John 20:15, the empty tomb:

"Woman, why are you weeping?"

This reminded me of the words from another Bible verse, Luke 24:5-6:

"In their fright, the women bowed down with their faces to the ground, but the angels said to them, 'Why do you look for the living among the dead? He is not here; He has risen!'"

By wallowing in the memories of the saddest days of our

lives—when our precious boy was taken from us—I wasn't allowing myself the joy of imagining Eric as he is now: in eternal life. These words caused me to think about what Jesus did for us by dying and rising from the dead; He opened the gates of heaven for us. Eric has walked through those gates and taken the place prepared for him in the kingdom of God, and this is something to rejoice and celebrate! Unfortunately, the reality of our existence here on earth sometimes makes that hard to do.

Mike

I find comfort in going to Eric's grave—praying there and caring for the flowers.

In February of 2011, I was hurting deeply. I went to Eric's grave daily and prayed that the Lord would somehow allow Eric to let me know that he was okay. My prayer became more insistent as I broke down, crying harder each day. However, I would always end my prayer by saying, "If this goes against Your will, I accept. But, if not, I would really appreciate it."

The Lord heard and answered my prayers.

Eric's headstone

On February 20, we received a call from the Rogalla family, whose son Nick had seen Eric in a vision the year before. They said they had news to share: Nick had been participating in a retreat when, once again, he experienced a vision of Eric during Eucharistic Adoration. But, this time, our boys spoke with each other! While looking at the monstrance, Nick experienced tunnel vision and saw a bright light emitting from the host on the altar; he was only able to see what was in front of him. Then, he saw a shadow coming from within the light and walking toward him. As the shadow got closer, Nick realized it was Eric.

Eric smiled at him and said, "Hey, Nick."

"Hey, Eric!" Nick replied.

"Nick, you have to do me a favor," Eric said. "Please, call my dad and tell him that I am okay; I am in heaven and I watch over him and all my family and will every day of their lives. But I need you to call and tell my dad that I'm okay."

Eric then spoke with Nick about some things that were just for Nick and ended the conversation by saying, "Be good, Nick. I will greet you when you cross. Have a good life."

After their talk, Eric walked back into the light and then the light faded away and all returned to normal. When I heard that Eric told Nick to let me know that he was okay, I was overwhelmed! No one—not even Laura—knew what I had been praying for every day for the last week. Nick lived more than 300 miles away from us; there was no way he could have known what I had prayed. I had specifically asked to hear those words. Little did I know when I prayed that prayer that the words would come from Eric himself!

Laura

Nick described what Eric looked like in his vision, saying, "Eric was wearing a white robe and the top of Eric's head glowed."

Shortly after receiving this phone call, I began reading the book, *Heaven is for Real* by Todd Burpo[3]. In it, he tells how his four-year-old son Colton began describing scenes from heaven and people he visited while there after his appendix burst. When I read Colton's description of the people he saw in heaven, I began to cry. It was the exact description Nick had given us of Eric!

August 7, 2011, was a Sunday, the day before our 25th wedding anniversary. We had requested that our marriage be blessed after Mass that day. Instead, we were called forward after communion so our marriage could be blessed before the entire congregation. We didn't help plan the music for this Mass, but we were pleasantly surprised by how the song selections and the readings spoke to us personally. The opening song was "How Firm a Foundation,"[4] which reminded me of the Gospel reading we had chosen for our wedding, Luke 6:47-48:

> *"I will show you what someone is like who comes to me, listens to my words, and acts on them. That one is like a*

person building a house, who dug deeply and laid a foundation on the rock; when the flood came, the river burst against that house but could not shake it because it had been well built."

I thought of the fact that the Lord is the foundation of our marriage and our life together. We also sang "Be Not Afraid"[5]. Our prayer group in Wisconsin had sung this for us as a farewell when we moved to South Dakota, and it speaks of trusting in the Lord in all our trials. In the closing song, "Be Still My Soul,"[6] the verses spoke to our hearts as though they had been written for us in that moment:

> *"Be still, my soul—the Lord is on thy side! Bear patiently the cross of grief or pain; Leave to thy God to order and provide. In every change, He faithful will remain. Be still, my soul—thy best, thy heavenly friend, through thorny ways leads to a joyful end.*
>
> *"Be still, my soul—thy God doth undertake to guide the future as He has the past; Thy hope, thy confidence let nothing shake. All now mysterious shall be bright at last. Be still, my soul—the waves and winds still know His voice who ruled them while He dwelt below.*
>
> *"Be still, my soul—the hour is hastening on when we shall be forever with the Lord, when disappointment, grief, and fear are gone, sorrow forgot, loves purest joys restored. Be still, my soul—when change and tears are past, all safe and blessed we shall meet at last."*

A few weeks later, on August 25, 2011—just a couple of weeks before the second anniversary of Eric's death—I was feeling the sorrow deeply and missing Eric intensely. Looking to the Word of

God for comfort, the pages of my Bible opened to Nehemiah 8:10:

> *"Do not be saddened this day for rejoicing in the Lord*
> *must be your strength."*

Since then, I have repeated that verse over and over in my mind. Rejoicing in the Lord must be our strength! Rejoicing in His love for us and in all that He has done and continues to do to show us how much He loves us. Everything we have is a gift from Him. I realized that I should always try to be grateful for the gifts I experience in life and not become possessive of them. I do not want to remain devastated by loss, but rather I want to feel thankful for the time I held the gift; I want to be focused on God's promises and the fulfillment of those promises in Jesus.

CHAPTER 14

Laura

To celebrate the landmark occasion of our 25th wedding anniversary, we were considering going on a pilgrimage to the Holy Land, and I prayed during Eucharistic Adoration to discern whether this trip was something God wanted us to do or if it was just something we desired. Seeking God's will in His Holy Word, I prayed and, as the Bible fell open, my eyes landed on Isaiah 66:13:

> *"As a mother comforts her child, so I will comfort you,*
> *in Jerusalem you shall find your comfort."*

This seemed like pretty strong confirmation that the Lord wanted this for us, so we decided to go. The pilgrimage was called, "In the footsteps of Jesus." For 10 days in October and November of 2011, we joined about 70 other pilgrims from the Diocese of Sioux Falls, South Dakota, led by Bishop Paul Swain, walking where Jesus walked. We celebrated Mass in the Church of the Annunciation in Nazareth and also in Bethlehem after kneeling at the site of our Lord's birth. We renewed our baptismal vows while being sprinkled with the waters of the Jordan River at the site of Jesus' baptism. We also had our marriage blessed by Bishop Swain in Cana of Galilee, where Jesus performed his first miracle—turning water into wine for the wedding feast at the request of His Blessed Mother, Mary.

One day, when I was feeling sick, Mike and the other pilgrims went to Capernaum and walked in the places where Jesus had proclaimed the Kingdom of God, healed the sick, and raised the dead. They experienced a boat ride on the Sea of Galilee and visited the Mount of the Beatitudes.

Later, we entered the tomb of Lazarus and celebrated Mass in the place where Jesus spoke the words that so comforted us the morning after Eric's death:

"I am the Resurrection and the Life. Whoever believes in me, even if he dies, will live." (John 11:25)

Our marriage is blessed in Cana of Galilee

In the Garden of Gethsemane, we picked up olive branches from trees said to be more than 2,000 years old, which means they would have been in the garden in Jesus' day. We also celebrated Mass in front of the stone on which Jesus wept the night before He died. And, finally, we walked the way of our Lord's suffering, carrying crosses on the Via Delarosa while praying the Way of the Cross.

. . .

The Holy Sepulchre is a huge building in Jerusalem that houses the locations of Christ's crucifixion, the stone slab on which His body was prepared for burial, and the tomb where Jesus was buried. We had been told that if we wanted to have some quiet prayer time in the Holy Sepulchre, we should go very early in the morning because the crowds arrive for Mass as early as 6 a.m. With this in mind, we left our hotel with another couple at about 4:10 one morning and walked the few blocks to the Holy Sepulchre. Very few people were there at that hour, and I asked a man if he could tell us where everything was located. He gave us the lay of the land and we began to explore. We entered our Lord's tomb and found a little chapel-like building above the tomb. When we went inside, we found ourselves in a small space that holds no more than 10 people and were later informed that this is where the angels announced to the women that Jesus had risen. Beyond that is the room where the tomb itself is located. This is a much smaller room in which only a few people can comfortably enter. The tomb is covered in marble, with a marble shelf above it.

As we went through the door into the first, larger room, we noticed that there were about eight people praying. Then, we looked into the tomb area and saw two women praying inside. We thought that the people out in the first space must be waiting for their turn to go into the tomb, so we began to pray while waiting our turn. Soon, a priest arrived and went into the tomb, and the two women came out and joined the rest of us in the outer room. Then, the priest joined us and began praying in Italian; we figured he must be leading them in morning prayer, so we kept praying, too. I could understand a little because of my musical training in college when, suddenly, I recognized words from the Mass. I looked at Mike and mouthed the words, "This is a Mass!" What a blessing to be present in our Lord's tomb for Mass! The priest prayed the Liturgy of the Word—the first part of the Mass in which we hear readings from the Bible—in the outer room with us. Then, he entered the tomb and prayed the Liturgy of the Eucharist—the second part of the Mass when Jesus gives Himself to us in Holy Communion. Catholics believe in the real presence of Jesus—body, blood, soul, and divinity—in the consecrated host. When the priest prays the words of consecration, the bread and wine on the altar actually become Jesus' body and blood. This is the very same sacrifice of Jesus on the cross on Calvary, made present in that moment. At the point in the Mass where the priest elevates the consecrated host, this priest turned to us, knelt down in the doorway of the tomb, and lifted the consecrated host for us to see. We knew the English words for what he was saying by heart: "Behold the Lamb of God who takes away the sins of the world. Happy are those who are called to His supper." We could see the consecrated host in his hands, Jesus truly present—body, blood, soul, and divinity—and only a few feet behind him, we could see Jesus' tomb. Here we were in the presence of our Lord Jesus in the very place where He rose from the dead, defeating sin and death! We responded with the words, "Lord, I am not worthy to receive you, but only say the word and I shall be healed!" I wish I could express in words what this moment meant to us. How awesome is our God! What an incredible moment of healing grace. *Thank you, Eternal Father God and our Lord Jesus, for allowing us to be blessed so abundantly by your love!*

The Lord reached out to us repeatedly on this trip and confirmed His love for us and the beautiful fact that our precious son is with Him in His Heavenly Kingdom. We remember these experiences with thanksgiving. There is so much for which to be thankful that it's sometimes difficult to express our gratitude. *God, you are so good! Thank you for all the gifts and blessings you have poured out on us over the years. We pray that all people will one day come to realize the depth of your love for them and turn to you in their need, surrendering their hearts and lives to you.*

. . .

There's no guarantee that if we are in a close relationship with God, we will not suffer. In fact, suffering is a part of our earthly existence; we can't escape it. In His earthly life, Jesus didn't sidestep suffering. He slogged through it, just as we do. However, knowing that we have a God who intimately understands what it is to suffer means that we have a companion in our life journey who can relate to our pain and comfort us.

Mike and Laura in Jerusalem at the Western (Wailing) Wall

In the summer of 2012, we went on a family camping vacation to a beautiful lake in northwestern Wisconsin. We stayed in a campground where our family had vacationed often when our children were growing up. Many times during those years, we celebrated Eric's birthday in this place, but I didn't want to be there on Eric's birthday this year because it was going to be very difficult to be there without him. Instead, we went a week later, and everywhere we looked brought back memories of the good times we had shared together in this place. The realization that we were moving forward and beginning to create new memories began to dawn on us as the week progressed. Yes, there was sadness in not having Eric present with us, but there were also moments of joy as we soaked in the fresh Wisconsin air and scenery. The time we spent together on this beautiful body of water was so refreshing and fun as we fished, boated, and swam.

And so, we go forward, embracing life as it presents itself. There will always be a place in our hearts reserved for Eric. I feel so thankful to the Lord for Eric's eternal life in heaven. Now, when I am missing him, I remember the dream I had of him in heaven and I find peace knowing that he is happier there than he could ever be here. I remember the joy on his face and I am able to accept that he belongs there now. Our faith tells us that, one day, when we depart this earthly life, we will be reunited with him. Staying focused on this fact—and the reality we've been shown of the life Eric enjoys in heaven—helps give us peace. We don't know what the future holds, but we know that, together with the Lord, we will face whatever comes, and we hope to continue growing to become all He intends us to be.

. . .

Mike gifted me with a pilgrimage to Medjugorje in April of 2013. This was his Christmas gift to me; I thought I was getting a pot and pan rack, but I liked the pilgrimage much better! I imagined that I would go and it would be a journey of thanksgiving. We have so much to be thankful for and I just wanted to be able to do that in Medjugorje. But God had other plans. As we climbed Apparition Hill and Cross Mountain, I kept seeing images of fish. Several rocks looked like fish, and one rock seemed to have the image of a fish carved out of it. Matthew 4:19 suddenly came to me:

"Come after me, and I will make you fishers of men."

Later that week during daily Mass, we heard about Jesus telling his apostles to cast their nets on the other side of the boat. When they do, they bring in a huge catch. Then, one day, as Stephanie led us in praying the Rosary, I had a vision. It began as my Cursillo vision did—with me as a little girl, walking barefoot up that grassy hill. Jesus met me at the top and sat down with me on His lap.

He looked into my eyes and said, "So, how are you doing?"

"Thank you for fixing my broken heart," I responded.

I placed my right hand, palm up, in front of my chest, my heart appeared on it and I showed it to Jesus. It was small, gray, and scarred. I felt ashamed of it; to me, it looked ugly. Jesus reached out and I placed my heart in His hand. Smiling, He looked at my heart.

Then, He said, "We are going to grow this together. By the power of my Holy Spirit, your heart will expand and you will love my children for me."

He placed my heart gently back in my hand and I saw light shining out through the scarred cracks. I placed it back in my chest and, hopping off His lap, I went to get Mike. I took Mike by the hand and led him to Jesus. As the two of them had their time together, I glanced around. When I looked toward the direction from which I had come, I saw the Blessed Mother Mary and Eric walking side by side up the hill. They were herding other little children up the hill to Jesus, and I noticed that there were children straggling behind them who were having a tough time getting up the hill. Mike and I joined hands, went down the hill, and got behind Eric and the Blessed Mother.

Then, we took these children by the hand and pulled them up the hill, encouraging them and saying, "Come to Jesus. You can do it! Come on, come to Jesus!"

This experience, along with others on that trip, gave me confirmation that Mike and I were supposed to share our experiences and try to help others in their faith journey, as well as help people to heal from tragic loss.

Mike

I often feel the "nudge"—a Holy Spirit prompting—to share my conversion story with people. Sometimes, this nudge occurs at inopportune times. Once, shortly after I started my work in South Dakota, I was at work when I felt the nudge. My computer was acting up, doing something really strange, so I called an IT worker to look at it. The man came into my office and looked at the computer.

"I've never seen anything like this," he said. "What did you do?"

I, too, had never seen anything like this and had only turned on the computer. And, while he was working with it, there it was—the nudge. I thought, "God, I'm at work. I don't know this person. I should not talk faith at work. I don't want to do this right now!" Nevertheless, the nudge became unbearable, persistent, and stronger— the confirmation that it was from God. So, I "threw out the bobber" and mentioned something about faith. The guy bit, and I shared a little about my conversion story with him. Suddenly, the man broke down and began crying, and I got up and shut my office door.

When he had collected himself, he said, "Mike, I have been feeling really lost lately. I prayed that God would send someone to help me find my faith again. He did; He sent you!"

We talked a little while and then he turned back to my computer to continue working on it and there was no longer anything wrong with it; it never acted up again. This scenario has occurred many times over the years. I trust the nudges now; I know how to test them to be sure they are from God.

For example, one day, I was flying home from a business trip and was seated across the aisle from a young woman. Suddenly, I felt the nudge to share faith with her. "Really, God?" I thought. "I'm on a plane. This woman is a complete stranger! I don't want to do this right now!" I ignored the nudge, like Jonah in the Old Testament who refused to take God's message to the Ninevites. Instead, I closed my eyes and pretended to sleep. The plane began to taxi out for take-off, but the pilot's voice came over the loudspeaker: We were going back to the gate, and the passengers would have to exit the plane because there was a mechanical problem. While I was waiting in line to reroute my flight, I was standing next to the same woman and the nudge increased in intensity. So, I initiated some small talk with her, and when we were reseated on our next flight, the woman and I were again across the aisle from one another. Once again, the nudge was irresistible, so I threw out the bobber. The woman bit, and it turned out that she was interested in discussing faith. For the entire flight—at her prompting—I shared my conversion with the dreams and Medjugorje. Repeatedly, I asked if I should stop and she asked me to continue. I shared throughout the entire flight from Charlotte to Chicago. When we landed, she told me that she had been born Catholic, but had fallen away. I asked her if she thought I was a nutcase and she became serious. She shared that her father had recently asked her, "How is your relationship with the Blessed Mother?"

Quite some time passed and Laura had been pressing me to

work on this book, but I didn't feel the nudge to do so; I believe the timing was not yet according to God's plan. I could sense her frustration, and while at Eric's grave praying, I asked God to guide me to do His will. I explained how I knew that, someday, we must share our story in a more public and broad way, but how I did not feel it from Him yet. I asked him to show me if I was doing His will in some way that I couldn't see. The next day, I was working late and I received an unrecognized email. I was about to delete it because I didn't know the sender, but then I saw the subject: Medjugorje. I opened the email and it was from the woman whom I had met on the flight from Charlotte. She started out by saying, "You probably don't remember me, but I met you on the flight from…" To make a long story short, she emailed me to let me know she was going to Medjugorje with Stephanie, and she wanted to let me know that it was because of my talk with her. She went to Medjugorje and experienced her own amazing conversion!

Later, in the summer of 2013, Laura and I called Stephanie one day to chat. During the course of our conversation, Stephanie mentioned that I was on her list to pilgrimage with her to Medjugorje that September. However, I couldn't remember signing up for the trip and Stephanie didn't know how I got on the list. At the time, Laura had been pestering me about writing this book, but I couldn't get myself to sit down and do it; Stephanie felt that when I went with her on this trip, whatever was blocking me from being able to write would be removed.

As it turned out, a woman from Sioux Falls, South Dakota, and I traveled to Split, Croatia, together. There, we would meet up with the rest of Stephanie's tour group. While in flight, I met several pilgrims from other tour groups who were also headed to Medjugorje. Once again, I received the nudge to talk about faith with the person next to me on the flight, and other people overheard the conversation, as well. It seemed as though God had arranged this situation, as a number of these people had lost a loved one to suicide, and my message of hope and healing was a comfort to them. I also met a young priest from another tour group, as well as several other pilgrims whom I would bump into repeatedly while in Medjugorje. Many times during this pilgrimage, I was invited to join different tour groups to share my conversion story; as a result, the members of my own group began to wonder who I was that so many people seemed to know me!

In Medjugorje, I had a very healing experience when Stephanie led our group in a healing Rosary. Soon after we began praying, I felt the Blessed Mother Mary on one side of me and Eric on the other, and I felt each of them place a hand on my shoulders. It felt so real and I believed it to be true; but, even with the many experiences I have had, I still questioned the reality of this type of experience and wanted confirmation. So, I prayed that the Lord would confirm the reality of this experience by having Stephanie see this, as well, and her letting me know she did. After we finished praying, Stephanie shared with our group the different things she had seen during the Rosary, but she did not share anything regarding my experience. I remember thinking that I believed it to be real and that, perhaps, God wanted me to just believe, so I accepted it. However, as the group filed out of the room, Stephanie took me aside. She said that during the Rosary, she saw the Blessed Mother and Eric each place a hand on my shoulders, and that she saw Eric on my right and the Blessed Mother Mary on my left—just as it had happened! What a confirmation this was!

Then, Eric made his presence known once again when our group climbed Cross Mountain. When we began the climb, I was near Stephanie and I noticed that she seemed to be having a very difficult time; she was breathing heavily, and I was concerned that she might not make it to the top of the mountain. So, I prayed silently to Eric, asking him to help Stephanie if God would allow it. Suddenly, I could hardly keep up with her!

At one point, Stephanie turned to me and said, "Mike, Eric is with us! He is helping me climb!"

Stephanie mentioned that when she sees Eric, he is "really, really big!" She thinks that this signifies his power as an intercessor and that he intercedes for each of us. Likewise, we believe that because several people have shared with us that God has a job for Eric, perhaps part of that job is interceding for other people—especially youth who suffer depression, despair, and bullying as he did.

One day during this pilgrimage, I felt a sudden strong urge to go to confession. Prior to the trip, I had prayed that God would provide me the confessional priest I needed—thinking this would be an older, very wise priest for this confession.

As I was hurrying on my way toward the confessionals, I heard someone call, "Hey, Mike!"

It was the young priest, Father William, whom I had met on the flight to Medjugorje.

We chatted for a bit when Father William, who was a newly ordained priest, said, "May I ask where were you headed? You seemed to be in a big hurry!"

I told him that I was on my way to the confessionals.

Father William had his stole draped over his arm and, pointing to it, said, "I just finished hearing confessions. If you'd like, I can open up a confessional and hear yours."

I hesitated for a moment. Father William wasn't exactly the priest I had been thinking of when I prayed for God to provide one for me. Then, I realized that this situation couldn't be a coincidence and that God had set this up.

So, I said, "Sure, that sounds great."

I began to confess what I had confessed so many times before—the many tormenting memories of things I had and had not done in my relationship with Eric, which I now regretted.

Father William said, "Let me ask you something, Mike. Do you think that what you are feeling is guilt, or do you think it might be shame?"

I hesitated for a moment pondering the question and then said, "I don't know. I think I'd have to look up the definitions of shame and guilt. I'm not sure I know the difference."

Father William said that the two may seem to be similar, but that they are actually quite different.

He went on to explain, "Guilt comes from God. It is a feeling God places on your heart, which may come from your conscience, your guardian angel, the Holy Spirit telling you that you have purposely done something against God's will. That you knowingly and willingly sinned against God. It's God's effort to bring you back to Himself.

"Shame is from the devil. It is the evil one trying to make you feel bad about yourself. He makes you dwell on memories that keep you imprisoned in fear and pain. It's the devil's effort to distance you from God. It makes you feel the guilt and shame of a sin, but you did not sin. You did not knowingly or willingly sin against God. Mike, you should look up the definitions of guilt and shame when you have a chance, but it sounds to me like what you are dealing with here is shame. The devil has been playing with you for quite some time, and I will now lay hands on you and cast the demon away!"

Father William prayed over me and I could feel this presence leave me. I finally felt peace and joy—nearly five years after the death of my son Eric. I left that confessional feeling like a huge weight had been lifted from my shoulders, and I haven't been plagued by those memories since! Later, I remembered that, while I was preparing for this pilgrimage, I had the feeling that I would battle the devil in some way on this trip. And I realized that the battle I had anticipated had occurred in that confessional. I will always be grateful for the healing experience I received from Jesus through Father William.

MOVING ON

Laura

We struggled in deciding whether to write this book; we even considered writing it anonymously because we don't want to draw attention to ourselves. But we realized that, in order to give credit to God for all He has done in our lives in a believable way, we had to be willing to put our names on this and stand up for the validity of what we have written.

We've shared here in all honesty the occurrences of grace that we have experienced up to this point in our lives. We hope that by sharing our experiences, others will begin to look for God working in their lives to draw themselves closer to Him. It's important to have your antenna up so you recognize what God is doing in your life; you can pray and ask God to help you clearly see the ways He is working for, in, and through you.

We couldn't have survived the loss of Eric and gone on to find hope in life again without the many ways that God reached out to us. What's more, our marriage would not have survived Eric's death if God had not brought Mike into relationship with Him through conversion. And, we wouldn't have been able to see those attempts by God to help us heal if we hadn't been looking for them.

We'd like to encourage each person who reads this book to look for ways the Lord is working in your life. Be aware that He thirsts for a relationship with you. As Jesus says in Matthew 7:7:

"Ask and it will be given to you, seek and you will find,
knock and the door will be opened."

Ask, seek, knock. You, too, will be amazed at the ways God answers when you turn to Him in prayer. Every day holds opportunities for all of us to reach our arms out to our loving Father God as His precious children; He wants to be in deep relationship with each of us. Just like the father in Jesus' story of the Prodigal Son (Luke 15:11-32), God—our Eternal Father—is watching for us to return to Him. He longs for us to reach out to Him so that He can lavish His love on us. He continuously invites us to be partakers in His divine love.

One of the songs inspired by the Holy Spirit that I wrote is called "Like a Pearl."[1] The lyrics of this song show how God views each of us as a precious treasure and how much He wants us to recognize His love for us:

"Like a Pearl"
© 2003 Laura Kondratuk

Refrain
Like a Pearl within an oyster, hiding deep within your heart is the
Spirit of the Lord
Just waiting, wanting to shine out.
The rough and rugged shell encloses a valued, priceless jewel,
And to crack this shell you have only to ask the Lord.

Verse 1
Man sees the beauty in the earthly things he has made.
He wants to protect and keep them for a very great price has been
paid.
His soul has been traded and his salvation lost.
But can he really understand the terrible cost?

Refrain

Verse 2
God sees the beauty in every heart He has made.
He wants to protect and keep you for a very great price has been
paid.
His Son died for you, for the salvation of us all,
and paid the ransom for our souls with His precious blood.

Final Refrain
Like a Pearl within an oyster,
Hiding deep within your heart is the Spirit of the Lord
Just waiting, wanting to shine out.
The rough and rugged shell encloses a valued, priceless jewel,
And to crack this shell you have only to ask the Lord.
Yes, to crack this shell you have only to ask the Lord!

. . .

Look at your life; have you noticed emptiness within you? That emptiness can only be filled with the love of God. Ask Him to fill you with the gifts of the Holy Spirit that He knows you need. Seek His presence. Knock at the door of His loving heart. Turn to the Lord and He will fill you with His love, peace, and joy. You can begin to experience the Kingdom of God here and now. Surrender to His love, open your heart to Him, and welcome Him in. Your life will change for the better, and you will never be the same. May these verses remind you of how suffering can turn into joy.

"But the Lord's eyes are upon the reverent, upon those who hope for
his gracious help,
Delivering them from death, keeping them alive in times of famine.
Our soul waits for the Lord, who is our help and shield.
For in God our hearts rejoice;
In your holy name we trust.
May your kindness, Lord, be upon us: we have put our hope in you!"
(Psalm 33:18-22)

"Sing praise to the Lord, you faithful; give thanks to God's holy
name.
For divine anger lasts but a moment; divine favor lasts a lifetime.
At dusk weeping comes for the night; but at dawn there is rejoicing."
(Psalm 30:5-6)

Appendix

Unless otherwise noted, Scripture quotations are taken from:

The New American Bible with Revised New Testament and Psalms © 1991, 1986, and 1970 by the Confraternity of Christian Doctrine, Inc., Washington, D.C. All Rights Reserved.

The Catholic Youth Bible © 2000 by Saint Mary's Press, 702 Terrace Heights, Winona, MN, 55987-1320, www.smp.org. All Rights Reserved.

Cover photo by Laura Kondratuk
Authors photo by Katie Luze
Back cover photo by Stella Mar Films

All photos by Kondratuk family members unless otherwise noted.

Chapter 1
1.   Monaco, James V. and McCarthy, Joseph. "You Made Me Love You", 1913.
2.   "Bountiful Harvest" © 2003 Laura Kondratuk.

Chapter 2
1.   Biser, Shirlanne. Photo of yarn Jesus. Used with permission.

Chapter 5
1.   John and Jami Meilhan family. Used with permission.

Chapter 8
1.   Father Rod Farke's talk from Eric's wake service. Used with permission.

2.   Karen Thaler's reflection from Eric's wake service. Used with permission.

Chapter 10
1.   Soldo, Mirjana. *My Heart Will Triumph*, 12-16. Catholic Shop Publishing, 2016. Used with permission.
2.   Mignone, Frank. Laura and Julie outside St. James Church. Used with permission.
3.   Mignone, Frank. Laura showing Julie miracle rock. Used with permission.

Chapter 11
1.   Joncas, Michael. 'On Eagle's Wings" Text: Psalm 91. New Dawn Music, 1979.

Chapter 13
1.   "Ode to Joy" text: Van Dyke, Henry; music: Van Beethoven, Ludwig; adapt. by Hodges, Edward.
2.   Neilsen, Randi. "A Person's a Person No Matter How Small" artwork. Used with permission.
3.   Burpo, Todd and Vincent, Lynn. *Heaven is for Real.* HIFR Ministries, 2010.
4.   "How Firm a Foundation" text: "K" in Rippon's A Selection of Hymns; music: Funk's A Compilation of Genuine Church Music, Winchester, VA, 1832.
5.   Dufford, Bob, SJ. "Be Not Afraid" text based on Isaiah 43:2-3; Luke 6:20. Text and music OCP, 1975, 1978, 2003.
6.   "Be Still My Soul" text: Von Schlegel, Katharina. Neue Sammlung Geislicher Lieder, 1752. Translated by Borthwich, Jane. Music: Sibelus, Jean.

Moving On
"Like a Pearl" © 2003 Laura Kondratuk.

About the Authors

Michael and Laura Kondratuk have been married for over thirty years and have three children and two grandchildren. Their youngest child died by suicide at age 14.

They enjoy spending time with family, traveling, fishing and just being together. Over the years, Michael and Laura have spoken to groups small and large, sharing their testimony of God's love and mercy. To contact for speaking engagements or information about their ministry, email ByGodsGraceKondratuk@gmail.com

Lightning Source UK Ltd.
Milton Keynes UK
UKHW012017200322
400364UK00007B/50